What God Has Joined Together

The Christian Case for Gay Marriage

DAVID G. MYERS AND

LETHA DAWSON SCANZONI

HarperSanFrancisco
A Division of HarperCollins*Publishers*

Also by David G. Myers:

The American Paradox: Spiritual Hunger in an Age of Plenty

Intuition: Its Powers and Perils

Also by Letha Dawson Scanzoni:

Is the Homosexual My Neighbor?
(with Virginia Ramey Mollenkott)

HarperCollins books may be purchased for educational, business, or sales promotional use. For information please write: Special Markets Department, Harper-Collins Publishers, 10 East 53rd Street, New York, NY 10022.

HarperCollins Web site: http://www.harpercollins.com

HarperCollins®, 📖®, and HarperSanFrancisco™ are trademarks of HarperCollins Publishers.

FIRST HARPERCOLLINS PAPERBACK EDITION PUBLISHED IN 2006

Library of Congress Cataloging-in-Publication Data is available.
ISBN-13: 978-0-06-083454-8
ISBN-10: 0-06-083454-4

06 07 08 09 10 RRD(H) 10 9 8 7 6 5 4 3 2 1

Praise for *What God Has Joined Together*

"I predict Myers and Scanzoni will influence readers to re-think their positions. These genuine bridge builders do a service to gays, to the faith community and to all of us who want a culture that supports families."
—Mary Pipher, author of *Reviving Ophelia*

"Provides a safe space for battle-weary warriors on both sides of the same-sex-marriage wars. The calm, comprehensive, convincing voices of Myers and Scanzoni create a safe place where all of us can hear again for the first time the truths that will lead at last to peace and reconciliation."
—Mel White, Soulforce.org

"A fresh and innovative approach to a controversial subject. Myers and Scanzoni make a persuasive case: If marriage is good for some, it's good for all."
—Nancy A. Hardesty, professor of religion, Clemson University, and author of *Faith Cure: Divine Healing in the Holiness and Pentecostal Movements*

"A very important 'first,' not only for the gay community but also for the Christian community. . . . I have been close to giddy with the hope and belief that this book may be the first significant break in the dam. . . ."
—Phyllis Tickle, religion editor (retired), *Publishers Weekly*

"Myers and Scanzoni argue that expanding the definition of marriage will strengthen it, not destroy it."
—*San Francisco Chronicle*

"Scanzoni and Myers argue that accepting gay marriage, far from threatening marriage, will confirm and strengthen the ideal of marriage itself for all of us, heterosexuals and homosexuals. Gay marriage can be a positive example for the many people in our society who hesitate and fear to embrace a permanent monogamous and lifelong relationship, with its struggles as well as its joys."
—Rosemary Radford Ruether, *National Catholic Reporter*

"A nice intro to progressive Christian perspectives on why 'reparative therapy' doesn't work, why the Bible isn't as antigay as Pat Robertson would have us believe, and why 'gay Christian' isn't an oxymoron."
—*Mother Jones*

"For anyone—especially serious Christians—interested in understanding the issues of marriage for same-sex couples, this book by Myers and Scanzoni is heartily recommended."
—*Evangelicals Concerned Review*

"*What God Has Joined Together* is strongest when Myers and Scanzoni are arguing for the virtues of Christian marriage and advocating that the same virtues be available to gay and lesbian couples."
—*Christian Century*

"An intriguing Christian argument for why same-sex marriage strengthens the institution of marriage."
—*Kansas City Star*, worthwhile books in religion

"The book is about a whole lot more than gay marriage. It's really about how to have civil discourse and how to think and talk with people who really disagree with you."
—*Hartford Courant*

"Scanzoni and Myers also offer a judicious tone by repeatedly stating that, regardless of political or religious differences, most people want a more family-supportive culture that values children, parenting and fidelity."
—*Virginian-Pilot*

"With all the recent chatter about the gay marriage debate circulating its way through the media, it's good to see a religious and pro-gay argument finally get its time in the spotlight."
—*Atlanta Jewish Life Magazine*

"An unexpected champion for gay marriage has emerged from this book: the devout Christian who firmly believes in the sanctity of marriage . . . for all peoples. Myers and Scanzoni ask difficult religious questions as they try to understand and bridge together the two sides of the debate: marriage-supporting and gay-supporting people of faith. Using the Bible, the two make a persuasive case for gay marriage, claiming that in a spiritual light, it is inherently beneficial."
—*Newcity Chicago*

"With its traditional defense of marriage and its progressive embrace of same-sex relationships, this book cannot be pigeonholed, and that in itself is refreshing."
—*Publishers Weekly*

Contents

In Appreciation

IF IT IS TRUE THAT "whoever walks with the wise becomes wise," then we are wiser for all the wisdom and advice received from our colleagues and friends. Although none of those to whom we are indebted bears any responsibility for what we have written, and most have differing views at one point or another, we are grateful for their guidance, correction, and encouragement. To Linda Bieze, Ralph Blair, Elizabeth S. Bowman, James Brownson, Kathryn Brownson, Philip M. Coons, Anne Eggebroten, Nancy Hardesty, Steven Hoogerwerf, Norman Kansfield, Rebecca Kiser, Heather Looy, Virginia Ramey Mollenkott, Carol Myers, Laura Myers, Kathryn Pigg, Martin Pigg, Alena Amato Ruggerio, David Scanzoni, Stephen Scanzoni, Suzannah Tilton, Barbara Timmer, David Van Heest, Allen Verhey, Clifford Williams, and Linda Williams, thank you.

Special thanks are due Kathryn Brownson for her wisdom, research, and assistance in manuscript preparation; to our agent, Susan Arellano, for connecting us to HarperSanFrancisco and being our occasional sounding board; to our discerning, patient, and supportive editor, Eric Brandt; and to Elaine Merrill and Carl Walesa for helping transform our work into a published book.

Credits

Bible Versions

A Personal Letter to Our Readers

THIS IS A BOOK about marriage. We believe in marriage. We want to see it strengthened. Knowing that strong, healthy, loving relationships are beneficial to the individuals involved and to any children they might have, we want to see couples flourish. We also believe that society, by supporting marriage, benefits as well.

In other words, we take marriage seriously. We affirm the solemn words of the traditional wedding ceremony in the *Book of Common Prayer* (1892), which asserts that marriage is holy and honorable and should not "be entered into unadvisedly or lightly, but reverently, discreetly, advisedly, soberly, and in the fear of God."

The ceremony tells us that marriage is a holy estate "into which these two persons present come now to be joined." From this time forward, they will be united in life's closest relationship. When they are asked, "Who is your nearest relative?" they will no longer give the name of mother, father, sister, or brother, but the name of this person, their spouse. They are now kin. They have made a commitment to love, support, comfort, encourage, and respect each other, helping each other to learn and grow and be all that they can be—separately and together. They will be there for each other in happy times, in hard times, and in the in-between ordinary everyday moments. They will have a partner in making decisions and sharing in the many pressures and responsibilities of modern life as well as in simply enjoying each other's companionship. In short, they are no longer alone. Ideally, this is what it means to be joined together by God in marriage.

And yet some who have yearned for such public commitment have been denied it. Over history, some couples have been barred from marriage for reasons of social class, race, or ethnicity. The burning question in our day is whether persons of the same sex should be prevented from sealing their love commitment in socially recognized marriage.

Many people have strong reservations about opening marriage to gays and lesbians. The reasons vary and may be rooted in politics, religion, ideas about gender, misinformation about sexual orientation, fear of societal change, or prejudice and bigotry. There may be other reasons as well. Voices have been raised to suggest that permitting persons of the same sex to marry will destroy the institution. We think not. We believe that opening marriage for gay and lesbian people could actually strengthen the institution for all people. In this book we will show why we believe that.

We not only take marriage seriously, we also take our Christian faith seriously. Among other things, this means that we approach this topic in a spirit of humility, knowing that we "see through a glass darkly" and that none of us has all the answers on this or any other subject. And we speak in a spirit of love, even toward those who vehemently disagree with us. We believe that "since God loved us so much, we also ought to love one another" (1 John 4:11), and we believe that this means respecting one another, even when we differ in how we interpret Scripture and understand God's working in the world.

The discussion we propose is not about winning arguments, nor is it about some abstract concept. It is about human beings, our brothers and sisters who are loved by God, whether they are heterosexual or homosexual. We bring to the discussion the conclusions we have reached, asking only that our readers be open to listening and to considering what we ourselves have been learning—and continue to learn.

And so we send out this book as an attempt to promote understanding and dialogue in the spirit of Jesus, who not only spoke of the oneness of two persons joined in marriage, but also prayed for oneness in the family of God: "I in them and you in me, that they may become completely one, so that the world may know that you have sent me and have loved them even as you have loved me" (John 17:23).

One

The Great Divide

How wonderful it is, how pleasant, for God's people
to live together in harmony!
—Psalm 133:1, TEV

A LONG-AGO SERMON recalled a time when the village church was burning. At the front of the bucket brigade was the town's atheist. "Why come now?" "Because the only time anything exciting happens here is when the church is on fire."[1]

Today's church is on fire, and the spectacle is agonizingly exciting. From across the battle lines, advocates and opponents of gay marriage and of gay ordination are throwing flames. Headlines express the passions: "180 Arrested in Protest over Church's Gay Policies"; "Fury As Church Appoints Gay Canon as New Dean of St. Albans"; "Church Gay Rift Widens"; "Conservative Methodists Propose Schism over Gay Rights"; "Presbyterian Battle over Homosexuality Still Unresolved."

The Reformed Church in America's general secretary, Wesley Granberg-Michaelsen, speaks for many denominational leaders when he says, "No issue today has as much potential to spawn divisiveness, mistrust, gossip, suspicion, and conflict in the church as this one. No issue has more capacity to confuse our focus, drain our energy, injure our fellowship, and divert our mission than this one. No current issue can so easily demoralize our meetings, paralyze our process, fuel our anxiety, and cripple our confidence as this one."[2]

Battles over ordaining gay and lesbian elders, deacons, ministers, priests, and bishops are but one front of this culture war.
Advocates for marriage renewal and advocates for same-sex
unions clash with passions that rival those surrounding the tax-
policy war, the job-outsourcing war, and even the war war. In
2004, eleven American states passed amendments banning gay
marriage. With more such amendments in the draft stage, and
with voices shouting both for and against a federal anti-gay-
marriage amendment, the passions are not subsiding.

"Barring a miracle, the family as it has been known for more
than five millennia will crumble, presaging the fall of Western civilization itself," observes an alarmed James Dobson, founder of
Focus on the Family. "For more than 40 years, the homosexual
activist movement has sought to implement a master plan that has
had as its centerpiece the utter destruction of the family."[3] The
approval of same-sex marriage by the Massachusetts Supreme
Judicial Court "is not just about homosexual rights," concurs
Charles Colson, Prison Fellowship founder. "It is even more
importantly about the death of marriage and family as we have
known it for thousands of years."[4] Colson calls the battle over the
definition of marriage "the Armageddon of the culture war."[5]
Same-sex unions "degrade" marriage, claimed Pope John Paul II.[6]
"Legal recognition of homosexual unions [would] obscure basic
values which belong to the common inheritance of humanity,"
contends a pope-approved statement by the Vatican's Congregation for the Doctrine of the Faith.[7]

"No one is waging war on marriage," responds *New York Times*
columnist Bob Herbert. "It's just the opposite. This is all about
people who are longing to embrace it."[8] Gay-marriage advocates
also point to a justice issue. "We have been together for 43 years,"
notes a gay letter writer to the *New York Times.* "Britney Spears was
married for 55 hours and had more legal rights than we ever
had."[9]

The fire that now is ripping through Catholicism and mainline
Protestant denominations likely will spread as attitudes change. In
but a thin slice of recent history, younger Americans' attitudes

have done an about-face. In 1978, 53 percent of entering collegians agreed that "it is important to have laws prohibiting homosexual relationships"; but among their 2004 counterparts, only 30 percent agreed with that statement.[10] Most Americans over age sixty-five oppose same-sex marriage, but most under thirty support it (see appendix B, "Attitudes Are Changing"), and from them will come tomorrow's church leaders. Sooner than you might expect, even conservative faith communities such as Southern Baptists may find themselves aflame. Generational succession is destiny.

Could it be that today's Holland, Belgium, and Canada—each of which now allows same-sex marriages—give us a glimpse of tomorrow's America? Are Vermont's civil unions and Massachusetts's legal same-sex marriages just the first beachhead of a social transformation that will sweep the nation as did the civil rights and women's rights movements in earlier decades?

James Dobson fears it. He writes that gay activist goals "that seemed unthinkable just a few years ago have largely been achieved or are now within reach. . . . We in North America and Europe are not simply 'slouching towards Gomorrah,' as Judge Robert Bork warned in his best-selling book; we are hurtling toward it."[11] On the other side of the divide, *New Republic* editor Andrew Sullivan finds himself "so surprised" by such conservative resistance. Allowing homosexual persons such as himself to marry "is the most pro-family measure imaginable—keeping families together, building new ones . . . [which] is why some elements of the old left once opposed such a measure."[12]

Bridging the Divide

Across the polarized church and nation, the debate rages. On one side are those who vigorously support marriage and marriage renewal. On the other are those who vigorously support everyone's right, regardless of sexual orientation, to seal love with commitment and to fully participate in the life of church and society.

We propose a third way, one that affirms, with evidence and conviction, *both* views. First, we aim to show why pro-marriage voices are right. Massive evidence reveals that *children, adults, and communities thrive where marriage abounds.* Liberals need to appreciate that conservatives such as Dobson have good reason for worrying that "the implications for children in a world of decaying families are profound."[13] Without insensitivity to the four in ten American adults who are unmarried, we need to step back and ask how we might create a more marriage-supporting social ecology—and, with it, happier and healthier people and flourishing neighborhoods.

Second, we aim to show why we marriage supporters can at the same time comfortably join many other heterosexual Christians in supporting the aspirations of gay and lesbian persons—and why we can do so not despite, but *because of,* our eagerness to renew marriage. We will, therefore, articulate the human need to belong. We will identify the benefits of secure, covenantal commitments. And we will offer a case for how gay marriage could help elevate the institution of marriage. (Actually, this book doesn't advocate a special type of marriage—"gay marriage"; it advocates strengthening *marriage,* and extending it as an option for another 3 percent or so of the population.) By so doing we hope to offer a bridge across the divide.* "Family values" and a biblically rooted faith can, we believe, happily coexist with supporting gay and lesbian persons' full participation in the culture and the church.

Along the way, we will offer a synopsis of what scientists have learned about sexual orientation (ours, yours, and everyone's). Is sexual orientation a chosen lifestyle? Aided by willpower, faith, or therapy, is it changeable? In attempting to answer such questions, we will aim to identify the emerging common ground shared by informed traditionalists and progressives. And we will highlight lingering issues that merit further research and dialogue.

This is not another book about homosexuals written by het-

---

* In this we are not alone. See http://www.bridges-across.org/.

erosexuals. (Gay and lesbian people don't need us to tell their stories.) Rather, in this book written by and for heterosexuals, we offer faith-informed and behavioral-science-informed reflections on sexual orientation, the human need to belong, and Christian sexual ethics. We will, for example, consider whether proposed state and federal amendments banning gay marriages would likely serve to strengthen or weaken support for heterosexual marriage.

We also will ask why passions about these issues run so strong. "What's the big deal?" we often hear. Why, for example, do the American Family Association and the Family Research Council argue so vigorously that supporting heterosexual marriage requires keeping homosexuals *un*married? Why do organizations that claim to be devoted to *family* issues disproportionately single out homosexuality for attention? Our February 2005 searches of the Focus on the Family, Family Research Council, and American Family Association Web sites revealed that each offers many more pages mentioning the word *homosexuality* or *homosexual* than mentioning "divorce." By contrast, the more marriage-focused National Marriage Project has zero Web pages mentioning *homosexuality* or *homosexual*.

The Authors

Given the passions surrounding the great divide over marriage and sexual orientation, readers will appropriately wonder about our experience, values, and biases. We (David and Letha) differ in gender and marital status, which gives us complementary sensitivities. David and his wife, Carol, have been married for forty-one years and are the parents of three adult children—two sons and a daughter. Letha experienced a painful midlife divorce after twenty-seven years of marriage and is the mother of two adult sons and the grandmother of three boys and two girls. Yet the two of us are kindred spirits as active Christians who care about compassion, love, and justice in the lives of all persons, regardless of sexual orientation.

We are committed to marriage and marriage renewal.
David serves on the advisory board of the centrist National Marriage Project. He was a contributor to and signer of the white
paper "The Marriage Movement" and its sequel.[14] To document
the post-1960 decline in child and family well-being and to make
the case for a marriage-supporting culture, he wrote *The American
Paradox: Spiritual Hunger in an Age of Plenty.* And he has spoken on
dozens of college and university campuses about commitment,
marriage, the social toxicity of pornography, and the human need
to belong.

Letha has coauthored three editions of a McGraw-Hill marriage and family textbook for college sociology courses. She has
written several other marriage-supporting books as well, including
*Sexuality, Sex Is a Parent Affair, Why Wait: A Christian View of Premarital
Sex, All We're Meant to Be,* and *Youth Looks at Love.* And she has spoken
at many churches, conferences, colleges, and seminaries on marriage and family issues.

Between us we have invested thousands of hours in supporting
marriage and family integrity. If you approach this book as a faith-
based marriage supporter, be assured: so do we.

**We value informed dialogue and support of our gay and
lesbian brothers and sisters.** Letha coauthored (with Virginia
Ramey Mollenkott) two editions of *Is the Homosexual My Neighbor? A
Positive Christian Response*, the first edition of which was published in
1978, when the Christian response was more often negative. In the
ensuing quarter century she has spoken to many groups as part of
her effort to educate, support, and provide resources to those who
are struggling to understand the truth about sexual orientation.

David has reported on sexual orientation in his introductory
psychology texts, in his book *Psychology Through the Eyes of Faith*, and
in his presentations. His published essay "Accepting What Cannot
Be Changed" has been visited by thousands on the Internet, some
of whom have written to tell him their stories. He also has served
as an interim adviser to the unofficial gay and lesbian student
organization at the college where he teaches.

Worshipping God with Our Minds

Throughout this little book, we will suggest areas of seeming common ground—points of possible agreement between informed people of faith on both sides of the divide. Toward that end, here is the first question we will ask ourselves: *Can we, whether we consider ourselves "conservatives," "liberals," or something else, find common ground in agreeing that Christians are called to worship God with their minds, and thus to love truth more than they love their own ideas?*

The life of faith is a dance on the boundary between conviction and humility.

Our *conviction* follows our leap of faith: we stake our lives on a biblically defined perspective that makes sense of the universe, that gives meaning and mission to life, that provides hope in the face of adversity and death. Conviction need not entail absolute certainty, but it does entail commitment. Sometimes, said the novelist Albert Camus, life calls us to make a 100 percent commitment to something about which we are 51 percent sure.

Our *humility* follows our conviction that we are not God. As a monotheistic religion, Christianity starts with two simple axioms:

1. There is a God.
2. It's not you (and it's not us).

These axioms imply our surest conviction: that some of our beliefs contain error. We are finite and fallible creatures. The reformers' motto—"reformed and ever-reforming according to the Word of God"—was mindful that none of us (and certainly not this book's authors) have a corner on God's truth. We all view reality in a dim mirror. Moreover, pride—thinking too highly of ourselves—is the deadliest of the seven deadly sins. Thus we need to hold all our ideas with a certain tentativeness as we humbly worship God with our minds by pursuing truth.

Historically, people of faith have pursued truth through the study of "special" and "natural" revelation—through the exploration of the following:

- the book of God's word (through our study of Scripture—our guide for faith and life);
- the book of God's works (our exploration of the creation).

As we believers approach difficult issues, our obligation is to be faithful to the creation. If God has written the book of nature, our calling is to read it as clearly as we can, remembering that we are answerable to the giver of all data for the accuracy of our observations. We do so always mindful that our biblical, theological, and scientific interpretations are vulnerable to error. All such human efforts are approximations that are subject to test, challenge, and revision.

Believing that both the biblical and natural data reveal God's truth, albeit filtered through human brains, we can listen to scholars who study Scripture or science. And we can allow biblical and scientific perspectives to challenge and inform each other. In humility we can also listen to one another's stories, perspectives, and insights. "Truth springs from argument among friends," observed the Scottish philosopher David Hume.

Sometimes the faith-mandated testing of our ideas *strengthens* them. Reading science, reading Scripture, and listening to others has, for example, strengthened our own conviction that children most often flourish when co-nurtured by adults who are enduringly committed to each other and to their children's welfare. It has strengthened our sympathy for marriage-supporting education, entertainment media, and economic policies. The evidence is overwhelming: Marriage matters.

Other times, the open-minded testing of our ideas *changes* our thinking. So it happened for us as we tested some of our earlier ideas about sexual orientation against the emerging evidence and the whole of Scripture. Research, reason, and people's life stories challenged us to revise our understandings. If change is discomfiting, as it has been for us at times, we can reassure ourselves with the advice of Marcus Aurelius: "Remember that to change thy mind and to follow him that sets thee right, is to be none the less a free agent." Indeed, Christian humility mandates the very opposite of fanaticism. (Fanatics, it has been said, are people who can't change their minds and won't change the subject.)

If we are to walk our talk—if our own thinking is to be ever-reforming—then what follows on these pages must be similarly subject to challenge and change. If all truth is God's, then we can all comfortably welcome debate and dialogue, challenge and change. That's what enabled the ages-long process by which the church has reformed its understanding of slavery, of women's roles, of what it means to have dominion over the earth—and even of marriage. Most people reading this book will not share their ancestors' Scripture-quoting support for arranged marriages and male headship, or their contempt for interracial couples and for those who have suffered divorce. With time, understandings change.

In eras past, the church has worked through other difficult science-religion questions as well. What is the earth's place in the universe? Was the creation a sudden, recent event or a long, slow process? What defines our stewardship over the creation—to master and subdue it, or to care for it? What is the appropriate place of women in the culture and in the church? A half century from now, the church and culture likely will have resolved the sexual-orientation question as well, and some of what is written here will seem antiquated. In her *Popular History of Astronomy During the Nineteenth Century*, published in 1893, Agnes Clerke recognized that today's tentative, searching understandings may to our descendants seem quaint:

> What has been done is little—scarcely a beginning; yet it is much in comparison with the total blank of a century past. And our knowledge will, we are easily persuaded, appear in turn the merest ignorance to those who come after us. Yet it is not to be despised, since by it we reach up groping to touch the hem of the garment of the Most High.

As faith-based people, we can perhaps agree that by adopting that ever-reforming and dialogue-supporting spirit of humility, we are taking the first step in bridging our divide. "Always be humble and gentle," we are reminded in Scripture. "Patiently put up with each other and love each other. Try your best to let God's Spirit keep your hearts united. Do this by living at peace" (Eph. 4:2–3, CEV).

Two

The Longing for Belonging

Happiness seems made to be shared.
—Pierre Corneille, *Notes par Rochefoucauld*

WE HUMANS HAVE a deeply rooted need to belong. We thrive in close, supportive, committed relationships. Appreciating the depth of this need may help today's people of faith bridge their great divide. In chapter 1, we asked whether a step toward bridging that divide might be an agreement that we are to love God and seek truth. We now need to ask ourselves a second question: *Can we agree that the yearning for closeness and connection is basic to covenant relationships?*

We are, said Aristotle, "the social animal." Massive evidence confirms what social psychologists Roy Baumeister and Mark Leary call our "need to belong."[1] Among our infant social responses—love, fear, anger—the first and greatest is love. Very soon after birth, we prefer familiar faces and voices. By eight months, we exhibit powerful attachments. We crawl after our caregivers and wail when separated from them. Reunited, we cling.

There is biological wisdom in this need to belong: It boosted our ancestors' survival. By keeping children close to their caregivers, attachments kept children out of harm's way. Adults who formed attachments were more likely to come together to reproduce, and to stay together to nurture their offspring to maturity.

Group bonds also enhanced survival. When hunting, six hands were better than two. When foraging, groups offered protection from predators and enemies. If those who felt a need to belong were therefore more likely to survive and reproduce, their genes would in time predominate. The inevitable result: a social animal. No wonder people everywhere on earth belong to groups and bond in close relationships.

And no wonder we bemoan fractured relationships. Uprooted to a foreign land, alone at a new school, isolated in prison, we ache over our lost connections. Even after being randomly thrown together at school, at summer camp, or on a vacation cruise, we lament the separation when parting. Hoping to sustain the new connections, we promise to call, to write, to come back for reunions.

If, as Barbra Streisand sings, "people who need people are the luckiest people in the world," then most people are lucky. Close relationships help satisfy our need to belong. And what you've heard is true: the closest relationship, marriage, is conducive to happiness, health, and freedom from poverty and to better educated, delinquency-free, thriving children. A recent report from the Commission on Children at Risk captures the point in its title: *Hardwired to Connect.*

Wanting to Belong

Our need to belong colors our thoughts and feelings. We can spend hours pondering our actual and fantasized relationships. When love relationships form, we feel joy. People falling in love sometimes have cheek aches from their irrepressible grins. When asked, "What is necessary for your happiness?" or "What is it that makes your life meaningful?" most people cite as their first answer close, satisfying relationships with family, friends, or romantic partners.[2] Happiness hits close to home.

When we feel included, valued, and loved by those important to us, our self-esteem rides high. Indeed, Mark Leary believes that self-esteem so closely mirrors our sense of belonging and being valued that it acts as a gauge that monitors our social connections.[3] To avoid rejection, win friendships, and sustain our self-esteem, we conform to expectations and strive to look and act in ways that make favorable impressions. We *need* to belong.

The Pain of Ostracism

Can you recall a time when your need to belong was thwarted by ostracism—when you felt ignored or excluded? What was it like to be shunned, to be avoided, to be met with averted eyes, even to be given the silent treatment?

Purdue University social psychologist Kipling D. Williams and his colleagues have studied ostracism—social exclusion—in both natural and laboratory settings.[4] Across the world, they report, humans use ostracism to control social behavior, with punishing effects. When ostracized, people respond with hurt feelings, anxious fretting, and a depressed mood. Those who've experienced the silent treatment from a family member or coworker have called it "emotional abuse" and "a terrible, terrible weapon to use." Lea, a lifelong victim of the silent treatment by her mother and grandmother, reflected, "It's the meanest thing you can do to someone, especially if you know they can't fight back. I never should have been born." During two years of silent treatment by his employers, reported Richard, "I came home every night and cried. I lost 25 pounds, had no self-esteem, and felt that I wasn't worthy."

If they feel rejected and unable to remedy the situation, people sometimes withdraw and sometimes turn nasty. In a series of studies, San Diego State University psychologist Jean Twenge and her collaborators told some participants that "everyone chose you as someone they'd like to work with."[5] They told the rest that the others *didn't* want them in their group. Compared with those who were told they were wanted, those excluded became much more likely to engage in self-defeating behaviors and to underperform on aptitude tests. They also exhibited more antisocial behavior, such as disparaging someone who had insulted them or, when given the option, blasting them with noise. "If intelligent, well-adjusted, successful university students can turn aggressive in response to a small laboratory experience of social exclusion," noted the research team, "it is disturbing to imagine the aggressive tendencies that might arise from a series of important rejections or chronic exclusion from desired groups in actual social life."

Most socially excluded teens do not commit violence, but some do. Charles "Andy" Williams, described by a classmate as someone his peers derided as a "freak, dork, nerd, stuff like that," went on a shooting spree at his suburban California high school, killing two and wounding thirteen.[6] The Columbine killers Eric Harris and Dylan Klebold were similarly on the fringes of their school's social networks.

Experiments have probed the ostracism effect. People who are left out of a simple ball-tossing game feel deflated and stressed. Kipling Williams and his colleagues were surprised to discover a toll even from "cyber-ostracism" by faceless people whom one will never meet. (Perhaps you have experienced this when feeling ignored in a chat room or when people neglect your e-mail.) Such ostracism elicits heightened activity in a brain area, the anterior cingulate cortex, that also activates in response to physical pain. Ostracism, it seems, *is* a real pain.

Williams and four of his colleagues personally experienced ostracism's effects in a little experiment on themselves, as each was ignored for an agreed-upon day by the four others. Contrary to their expectations that this would be a laughter-filled role-playing game, the simulated ostracism disrupted work, interfered with pleasant social functioning, and "caused temporary concern, anxiety, paranoia, and general fragility of spirit." To frustrate our need to belong is to unsettle our lives.

When prolonged, an unmet need to belong can foster depression. Martin Seligman, a past president of the American Psychological Association, notes that rates of depression have soared as kinship connections have waned.[7] He believes that depression is especially common among young Westerners because of the epidemic hopelessness that stems from the rise of individualism and the decline of commitment to faith and family. When facing failure or rejection, contends Seligman, the self-focused individual takes on personal responsibility for problems and has nothing to fall back on for hope. A well-connected person is a well-supported person. A lonely person is an unhappy person.

To be "wretched" literally means, in its Middle English origin (*wrecche*), to be without kin nearby. Indeed, children reared in institutions without normal social attachments or locked away at home under extreme neglect often do become wretched—withdrawn, frightened, speechless. After studying the mental health of homeless children for the World Health Organization, psychiatrist John Bowlby asserted that "intimate attachments to other human beings are the hub around which a person's life revolves" and that this is true in every stage of life from infancy to old age. He wrote that intimate attachments reciprocally provide strength and enjoyment to each individual in the relationship. "These are matters about which current science and traditional wisdom are at one."[8]

Among adults, jealousy, guilt, and loneliness all involve a disrupted need to belong. With their need to belong thwarted, the bereaved often feel that life is empty and pointless. Exile, imprisonment, and solitary confinement are progressively more severe forms of punishment.

Belonging and the Good Life

What makes for a good life—a happy and satisfied life? Repeated surveys of hundreds of thousands of people worldwide reveal who is happy. Happiness is about equally attainable for people of any age and of either gender (though when things go badly, women more often ruminate and become depressed or anxious, while men more often abuse alcohol or engage in antisocial conduct). Income is but a modest predictor of happiness. It's no fun to be abjectly poor. But the middle class and the rich are about equally happy. And as real income has doubled over the last half century— and with it all that money can buy—happiness has slightly declined. (It's shocking but true: economic growth in the United States and in other Western countries has *not* led to improved human morale.)

So who *is* happy? As David explains in *The Pursuit of Happiness,*[9] the good life springs less from earning one's second hundred thousand than from

- developing the *traits* that mark happy lives. (Happiness is optimism, positive self-esteem, and a sense of control over one's life.)
- finding connection and meaningful hope in *faith communities.* (In National Opinion Research Center surveys of forty-two thousand Americans, 26 percent of those rarely or never attending religious services declared themselves very happy, as did 47 percent of those who attended more than once a week.)
- enjoying the *"flow"* of work and recreation in which there is deep involvement. (Between the anxiety of being overwhelmed and stressed on the one hand and the apathy of being underwhelmed and bored on the other lies a zone in which people experience flow—an optimal state in which, absorbed in an activity, they lose consciousness of self and time. Most people are happier gardening than power-boating, happier talking to friends than watching TV.)
- above all, *loving and being loved.* To experience well-being, report the happiness experts Ed Diener (University of Illinois) and Martin Seligman (University of Pennsylvania), "people need social bonds in committed relationships."[10] People—all people, straight or gay—benefit from having soul-mate companions through the journey of life, people who are there for one another in times of celebration and in times of suffering and sorrow. A deep friendship, wrote the seventeenth-century sage Francis Bacon, "redoubleth joys, and cutteth griefs in half."

Mountains of data confirm that most people are happier attached. The institution of marriage has traditionally offered the possibility of forming one of life's deepest attachments. Social science research has shown that, compared with those who never marry, and especially with those who have separated or divorced, married people report greater happiness and life satisfaction. This marriage-happiness correlation isn't perfect (there are miserable married people and joyful singles). But it extends across countries and both genders (contrary to the pop psychology myth that marriage is a good deal for men and a bad deal for women). Over the past three decades in the United States, for example, 40 percent of married adults, and 23 percent of never-married adults, have declared themselves "very happy" (in a periodic government-financed social survey conducted by the University of Chicago's National Opinion Research Center).[11]

Why are married people happier? Does marriage breed happiness? Or do happy people more often marry and stay married?

The marriage-happiness traffic appears to run both ways. First, happy people, being more good-natured, outgoing, and sensitive to others, may be more appealing as marital partners. Unhappy people experience more rejection. Misery may love company, but company does not love misery. An unhappy (and therefore self-focused, irritable, and withdrawn) spouse or roommate is generally not much fun to be around. For such reasons, positive, happy people more readily form happy relationships.

Yet "the prevailing opinion of researchers," noted sociologist Arne Mastekaasa, is that the marriage-happiness correlation is "mainly due" to the beneficial effects of marriage.[12] And for good reason. Marriage entails new stresses, but also new sources of identity and self-esteem. With new roles—that of spouse and perhaps parent—our identity gains additional legs. Thus if we mess up at work, we can tell ourselves, "Hey, I'm a good wife and mother [or "husband and father"], and that's what really matters." Marriage also offers both an antidote to loneliness and the potential for enduring, supportive intimacy. A good marriage gives each partner a dependable companion, a secure and comfortable lover, an intimate friend.

Will these benefits extend to same-sex marriages as well? Studies done before the advent of twenty-first-century gay marriage reveal "striking similarities" in the love and satisfaction experienced by same-sex couples and heterosexual couples.[13] "Because involvement in a close relationship is linked to overall well-being," notes psychologist Lawrence Kurdek, "protecting same-sex relationships is tantamount to protecting the well-being of the partners involved in those relationships."[14] Before long, enterprising researchers may discover whether the marriage-happiness correlation extends to people in same-sex marriages. Given the panhuman need to belong, few will be surprised if it does.

Psychology's term for intimacy is *self-disclosure*—the sharing of private likes and dislikes, dreams and worries, proud and embarrassed moments. "When I am with my friend," reflected the Roman statesman Seneca, "methinks I am alone, and as much at liberty to speak anything as to think it." So it is in a happy marriage, where trust displaces anxiety and where one is free to be open without fear of losing the other's affection. Marriage at its best is intimate friendship sealed by commitment. Issues of rights aside, is it a wonder that marriage is a worldwide institution? Is it a wonder that most people, whether straight or gay, say they would like to marry?[15] Is it a wonder that popular romantic films—*Sleepless in Seattle, Bridget Jones's Diary, My Big Fat Greek Wedding, Sense and Sensibility*—portray the happy matrimonial satisfaction of our need to belong?

The covenant relationship called marriage exists because human beings were not meant to be alone. Upon marriage, "the two shall become one flesh" (Mark 10:8). But not everyone will experience such a "one flesh" relationship throughout their adult lives—or even at all. It's important, then, to remember that romantic, erotic love isn't the only kind of love, nor is it the only way to meet the yearning to belong. The word *intimacy* derives from a Latin term for "close friend." The emotional closeness we can experience in deep friendships offers the possibility of "one soul" relationships when "one flesh" relationships are not an option.

Ergo, to have your need to belong well met—to have people in your life who celebrate when you're born, care about you as you live, and will miss you when you're gone—is, very likely, to enjoy a good life.

Belonging and Health

Linda and Emily had so much in common. When interviewed by a UCLA health psychology team led by Shelley Taylor, both had married, raised three kids, suffered comparable breast tumors, and recovered from surgery and chemotherapy. But their situations differed. Linda, a widow in her fifties, was alone and without significant friends, her children scattered elsewhere. "Having no one with whom to share her thoughts on a daily basis," reported Taylor, "she unloaded them somewhat inappropriately with strangers, including our interviewer."

Interviewing Emily was difficult in a different way. Phone calls interrupted. Her nearby children were in and out of the house. Her husband called from his office for a chat. Two affectionate dogs roamed the house. Emily, said Taylor, "seemed a serene and contented person, basking in the warmth of her family."

Three years later, when trying to reinterview both, they learned that Linda had died, while well-connected Emily was as happy and healthy as ever.

We cannot be certain what led to Linda's and Emily's differing fates. But they illustrate a conclusion drawn from seven massive investigations, each of which followed thousands of lives through years of time: social support—feeling liked, affirmed, and encouraged by intimate friends and family—predicts a lessened risk of ill health and premature death.[16] It has long been known that married people, on average, live longer, healthier lives than the unmarried. One seven-decade-long Harvard study found that being in a good marriage at age fifty predicts healthy aging better than does a low cholesterol level at that age.[17]

Does the marriage-health correlation mean merely that healthy people more often marry and stay married? After controlling for various possible explanations, two recent analyses independently concluded that marriage supports health. Marriage "improves survival prospects"[18] and "makes people healthier and longer-lived."[19] This is especially true for happy and supportive (rather than conflict-laden) marriages.[20]

But why? Among the conjectured reasons are these: Given a supportive marital partner, people *receive medical attention sooner.* They *sleep better, cope better* with stresses, and find their *self-esteem bolstered* when wounded by others' slings and arrows. They also *eat better, exercise more, and smoke and drink less.* (One study of fifty thousand young adults found that unhealthy behaviors dropped sharply after marriage;[21] another study of thirty thousand men found that when a marriage ended, vegetable consumption plummeted and fried food and alcohol consumption spiked.)[22] "Woe to one who is alone and falls and does not have another to help," noted the author of Ecclesiastes.[23]

A well-satisfied need to belong also supports stronger immune functioning. Social ties even confer resistance to cold viruses, report the University of Pittsburgh psychologist Sheldon Cohen and his colleagues.[24] They discovered this after administering nasal drops laden with a cold virus to 276 healthy volunteers before putting them into quarantine for five days. (The sometimes sniffly volunteers were lured by a payment of eight hundred dollars apiece.) Even after controlling for age, race, sex, and smoking and other health habits, the link between strong social ties and fewer resulting colds was nothing to sneeze at. Moreover, dozens of other studies reveal that social ties calm the cardiovascular system and lower blood pressure and levels of stress hormones.[25]

Unlike most fleeting "hook-ups," our close, intimate relationships enable us to confide painful feelings. University of Texas health psychologist James Pennebaker has studied the healing power of "open heart therapy"—talking out problems. In one study, he and his colleagues contacted the surviving spouses of people who had committed suicide or died in car accidents. Those who could talk through their grief had fewer health problems than those who bore it alone.[26] In another study, thirty-three Holocaust survivors spent two hours recalling their experiences, often in intimate detail never before disclosed. In the weeks that followed, most showed family and friends a videotape of these recollections. As in other studies, those who were most self-disclosing enjoyed the most improved health fourteen months later. Confiding—the

heart-to-heart disclosure enabled by secure and intimate relationships—is good for soul and body.

The bottom line: We humans have a fundamental need to belong. We
thrive in close, supportive, committed relationships. Marriage is a
very special committed relationship, and where marriage abounds,
we (and, as we'll see, our children) are often happier and healthier.
As the Christian author C. S. Lewis said, "The sun looks down on
nothing half so good as a household laughing together over a
meal."[27]

This reality has implications for our personal lives and our
public policies.

At a personal level, it encourages our seeking or sustaining a
life partner. It compels us to nurture our closest relationships: to
not take those closest to us for granted; to display to them the sort
of kindness that we display to others; to affirm them; to play
together, pray together, and share together.

At a public level, it mandates what the next two chapters envi-
sion—a more marriage-supporting social ecology. Given that well-
being "rests on strong family and friendship ties," say Ed Diener
and Martin Seligman, "we would argue that government policies
should be aimed at cementing strong social ties. This could mean
offering tax breaks to married couples (a conservative proposal),
and it could mean adopting marriage for gay and lesbian couples
(a liberal position)."[28]

Regardless of whether one tends to favor the conservative or
the liberal position—or both (by viewing the marriage option as
healthy for all)—there seems a near consensus on this much: we
are made to belong. When someone "loves you for a long, long
time," explained the wise old Skin Horse to the Velveteen Rabbit,

> "not just to play with, but REALLY loves you, then you
> become Real."
> "Does it hurt?" asked the Rabbit.
> "Sometimes," said the Skin Horse. . . .
> "Does it happen all at once . . ." he asked, "or bit by bit?"

"It doesn't happen all at once," said the Skin Horse. "You become. It takes a long time. That's why it doesn't often happen to people who break easily. . . . Generally, by the time you are Real . . . you get loose in the joints and very shabby. But these things don't matter at all, because once you are Real you can't be ugly, except to people who don't understand."[29]

Adults as well as children identify with this story. Created to be social creatures, we find we're most "real" in connectedness to others. At the core of our beings—our innermost selves—we long to feel special, understood, cared about. Loving and being loved makes us feel recognized, that we matter, that we're *real*. South Africans have a word for these human bonds that define us all. *Ubuntu* (oo-BOON-too), explains Desmond Tutu, expresses the fact that "my humanity is caught up, is inextricably bound up, in yours."[30] A Zulu maxim captures the idea: *umuntu ngumuntu ngabantu*—"a person is a person through other persons."

Three

The State of Our Unions

*The ranks of optimists who think the family is alive and well
have thinned considerably.*
—Arlene Skolnick, *Embattled Paradise*

"GOD SETS THE LONELY in families," said the psalmist (Ps. 68:6, NIV). We need the connectedness that a family provides. Sometimes that sense of belonging comes from someone else's family welcoming us with open hearts and arms. Often close friends serve as God's remedy for aloneness by providing a feeling of family. (Some single persons can attest to the truth of Proverbs 18:24: "A true friend sticks closer than one's nearest kin.") In biblical times, the family was defined more broadly than in our culture today. The emphasis was on a *household,* with many persons, both related and unrelated, living under the same roof. The New Testament also emphasizes the family of believers: the church. Still, for most people today, the word *family* conjures up an image of couples and children bonded to each other socially and legally through marriage, birth, or adoption.

Marriage, observed the anthropologist George Murdoch on the basis of his cross-cultural studies, has two ingredients that together separate it from other relationships: economic interdependence and sexual interdependence. A third ingredient—a socially recognized contract—involves a special license sealed by a public commitment. Whether the public ceremony takes place before witnesses at a courthouse, in a house of worship, or during some other festive celebration, society declares that this relationship is more than a private matter between two individuals. Marriage is an interdependent relationship that entails both rights and responsibilities.

Whatever our differences, most of us people of faith would welcome a more marriage- and family-supportive culture, one that

- welcomes children into families with parents that love them, and into an environment that nurtures families;
- encourages close relationships within extended families and with supportive neighbors and caring friends;
- values our diversity while finding unity in shared ideals;
- develops children's capacities for empathy, self-discipline, and honesty;
- provides media that offer social scripts of kindness, civility, attachment, and fidelity;
- regards sexuality as life-uniting and love-renewing;
- encourages spiritual awareness of a reality greater than the self and of life's resulting meaning, purpose, and hope.

Whether liberals or conservatives, feminists or fundamentalists, we share these values. With such common values and aspirations agreed upon, could we engage in a national dialogue about how best to realize them? Could we affirm liberals' efforts to reduce the demoralizing effects of poverty and also affirm conservatives' efforts to encourage positive media? Could we affirm liberals' support for family-friendly workplaces and also affirm conservatives' support for marriage? Could we affirm liberals' advocacy for children in all sorts of families and also affirm conservatives' support for co-parenting?

Marriage Matters

This vision—of a world with well-connected adults whose culture supports their co-parenting of flourishing children—has been challenged by a widely recognized social recession. In a 2004 survey of Americans by the Gallup Organization, "the overall state of moral values" was judged less than "excellent" or "good" by eight in ten Republicans, and also by eight in ten Democrats.[1] Of special concern is the abrupt decline of marriage and co-parenting. We are living longer and loving shorter.

Let's make this precise. Since 1960, a mere eyeblink of historical time,

- the average woman's age at first marriage has jumped from twenty to twenty-five, the average man's from twenty-three to twenty-seven;
- the marriage rate (the annual number of marriages per one thousand unmarried women) has fallen 38 percent;
- the number of couples cohabiting has soared from 0.4 million to 5 million;
- the proportion of never-married twenty-five to twenty-nine-year-old women has soared from one in ten to four in ten, while the proportion of unmarried thirty-five to forty-four-year-olds tripled from one in ten to three in ten.

So, since 1960 we're not only divorcing more—each year there are 2.2 million marriages and half that many divorces—we're postponing marriage, marrying less, cohabiting more, and also living alone more. For all these reasons, we're much less likely to be connected to a life partner. The unmarried proportion is up 64 percent (to four in ten adults over age eighteen). With 86 million single adults, there has been an understandable boom in singles bars, singles ministries, singles housing, and singles cruises.

With so many more singles, the stigma associated with being single has lessened. Given that not everyone is destined to marry, we can welcome the change and be glad for the fulfilling lives that many singles report. "It's a different kind of happiness," says Barbara Feldon, the author of a book on singleness. "It's different than mated happiness, but it is still happiness."[2]

But simultaneously, the association of sex with commitment has also lessened. Recreational sex—people enjoying one another's bodies—has become, in the words of a Broadway song, "the friendliest thing two people can do." "If two people like each other, it's all right for them to have sex even if they've known each other for a very short time," agreed 46 percent of entering collegians in 2004.[3] In today's world, such "hook-ups" are commonly modeled by the media and often fueled by alcohol. Meanwhile, since 1960, the percentage of children born to unmarried parents has mushroomed from 5 to 33 percent. (Married women are having fewer children, and the increasing number of unmarried women, despite easier access to birth control and abortion, are having more.) So—no surprise, given all these trends—the proportion of children who are not co-parented has surged from roughly one in ten to three in ten.

Even many champions of the traditional family as depicted by Norman Rockwell have lived otherwise. Ronald Reagan divorced the mother of two of his children (to whom he was a distant parent) and married Nancy, who bore their first child seven and a half months later. Newt Gingrich divorced his wife, who was ill with cancer. Rush Limbaugh has married and divorced three times. Bill O'Reilly settled a sexual-harassment suit. And several family-values champions in Congress have failed to walk their talk. The conservative moralist Dan Burton acknowledged fathering a child out of wedlock. The Defense of Marriage Act, noted columnist Nicholas Kristof, was "written by the thrice-married Representative Bob Barr and signed by the philandering Bill Clinton. It's less a monument to fidelity than to hypocrisy."[4]

Judging Versus Understanding

A cautionary note: when our attention is drawn to someone's misbehavior, it's tempting to blame the person and to ignore the history and the situation that helped breed such behavior. When American guards brutalized Iraqi prisoners, the first response was to blame the "bad apple" guards and to ignore the barrel in which those apples festered—the corrupting power of war and prison life. As America's obesity rate has doubled since the late 1970s, it has been tempting to blame individuals for their choices—"their fat is their fault"—and to ignore the environment that makes us more likely to lose the battle of the bulge. Likewise, it's tempting to blame individuals for the rise in impermanence, infidelity, and hooking up and to ignore its origins in the culture's radical individualism and its media models of impulsive sexuality. The moral: It's understandably tempting to swat the mosquitoes (and individuals need not be absolved of responsibility). But it's more effective to drain the swamps. Better to prevent than to judge.

With divorce, the cultural-swamp factor is big. Some powerfully toxic forces have been at work to account for the post-1960 doubling of the divorce rate (despite people's marrying later and after more schooling, which lessens the divorce risk). Many who suffer divorce have been victimized by a partner's abandonment, adultery, cruelty, or knavery. In such intolerable situations, divorce may provide a first step toward healing and a saner environment for one's children. Divorce is like an amputation. It's bad news, the remedy of last resort, and something we all hope to avoid. (Greeting-card companies trivialize the agony and frequent loneliness: "Getting divorced can be very healthy! Watch how it improves your circulation!" offered a Hallmark card.)[5] But sometimes amputation is a lesser evil than retaining a hopelessly diseased limb. To say that health and commitment are *ideals* is not to judge those with broken limbs or broken marriages.

And if people of divorce have known brokenness, who among us has not? We are, all of us, earthen vessels. We all at some time find ourselves broken—if not in our love life, then in our parenting, our friendships, our vocations, or our bodies. Within David's and Letha's own extended families, we have witnessed much love, laughter, and good fortune, but also depression, divorce, premature death, attempted suicide, and estrangement. Let those who are without brokenness cast the first stone.

Does Marital Decline Matter?

The philosopher Bertrand Russell once said that the mark of a civilized human is the capacity to read a column of numbers and weep. Do the statistics of marital decline merit weeping? Should they motivate a social renewal movement, perhaps comparable in scale to the earlier civil rights, women's, and environmental movements? Or, as the Alternatives to Marriage Project contends, is it all for the better? (On the project's list of favorite quotes: "If marriage isn't a prison, why do they call it wedlock?") After all, Oprah Winfrey and Stedman Graham seem happily coupled without being married. Susan Sarandon and Tim Robbins have not considered legal marriage necessary for their longtime relationship as devoted partners and parents. When Madonna was four months pregnant with her first child (after her fitness instructor performed "the father gig"), her publicist reported her "deliriously happy." And on HBO, Samantha Jones's sex in the city sure looked glamorous. (Never mind that two-thirds of sexually experienced American teens, including almost four in five girls, later wish they had waited longer before becoming sexually active.)[6]

Let's make the questions more specific:

With people freer to leave miserable marriages, aren't surviving marriages happier? Guess again. As divorce was increasing during the 1970s and into the 1980s, the percent of "very happy" marriages was declining and reports of marital conflict were increasing.[7] Bad marriages were more often ending, and marriages were more often going bad.

Research on what Swarthmore College psychologist Barry Schwartz calls "the tyranny of choice" helps explain why freedom to escape bad marriages might, ironically, lead to decreased marriage satisfaction. Freedom is great to a point, beyond which we begin agonizing over excess choices and then ponder, with regret, the attractive unchosen alternatives. (One recipe for marital unhappiness includes continually comparing one's partner with potential other partners.) When feeling bound to something or someone, we're more likely to love it than when we are freer to contemplate alternatives. Regard something as forever yours, and you are more likely to love it.

Don't cohabitations—"trial marriages"—weed out unsuccessful or risky unions before marriage? Aren't we happier with cars (and marriages) that we test-drive before buying? Most young Americans think so. Six in ten American high school seniors agree or "mostly agree" that "it is usually a good idea for a couple to live together before getting married in order to find out whether they really get along"; only one in four disagrees.[8] Among the thirteen- to seventeen-year-olds questioned in a 2004 Gallup survey, seven in ten approved of "couples living together before they married."[9]

So, is cohabitation to marriage what spring training is to baseball?[10] Alas, the myth crashes against a wall of data. Cohabitation surely spares us some ill-fated marriages, and might have spared us some of Elizabeth Taylor's eight marriages. "I always thought I had to get married," she has reminisced. "That's passé now."[11] But what about those who, after a seemingly successful trial marriage, do decide to marry? Ten large studies across several countries concur that, compared with couples who don't cohabit with their spouses-to-be, those who do have *higher* divorce rates.[12]

New data suggest a possible exception: when the prenuptial cohabitation is postengagement and exclusive to one's future spouse, the risks may diminish.[13] But in general, a successful trial marriage is a statistical predictor (though not a fatalistic predictor) of a future failed marriage. So what explains this cohabitation-divorce correlation?

Here's one explanation: people who cohabit bring a more individualistic ethic to marriage. They are more likely to see close relationships as temporary and fragile, are less sure that marriage is right for them, are more accepting of divorce, and are about three times more likely after marriage to have an affair.[14] To put it bluntly, the sort of person who would readily cohabit with you is a person who, when the romance fades, might be unfaithful and eventually leave you. Sociologists call this a *selection* effect .

There is also a second factor at work: the *causal* effect. The experience of cohabitation *decreases* endorsement of marriage and *increases* acceptance of divorce.[15] Over time, those who cohabit without marriage become more approving of dissolving an unfulfilling union. This divorce-accepting attitude increases the odds of later divorce. (It also doesn't help that people who cohabited before marriage rate their marriages as less satisfying.)[16]

And there's more bad news for the myth that trial marriages are socially useful. Some nine in ten first cohabitations are impermanent.[17] Even when children are born to the cohabitants, three in four of those children will by age sixteen suffer their parents' breakup (as will only a third of children born to married parents). When the relationship ends, cohabitation—a no-strings-attached arrangement—has tended to be a bad deal for women in that it enables their male partners (who usually earn more and keep separate checking accounts) to walk away with most of the partnership's assets. A live-in boyfriend who is not the biological father of a woman's children also puts her kids at increased risk of physical and sexual abuse.

Cohabiting partners typically have as active a sex life as do married folks. But they're less likely to report their sex to be physically or emotionally satisfying and more likely to report violent arguments and assaults. They're also more likely to suffer from a partner's unfaithfulness. And they're just plain unhappier and more vulnerable to depression.[18] All in all, concludes University of Chicago sociologist Linda Waite, cohabitation "may represent a new enslavement rather than freedom for women."[19] The media modeling of cohabitation—"commitment with one's fingers crossed," as marriage advocate Maggie Gallagher calls it[20]—may have helped persuade most teens that it's "a good idea." But in truth, the data suggest, it's a bad idea. More often than not, cohabitation is a union that defies management.

Don't children tend to benefit from the termination of toxic, stressful marriages? Indeed, some children *are* better off when their mothers (or fathers) escape a conflict-ridden or abusive marriage, sometimes to an alcoholic spouse. In the words of West Virginia University psychologists Patrick Davies and Mark Cummings, "Destructive forms of marital conflict undermine children's feelings of emotional security."[21]

Couples, however, are usually more painfully aware of their marital conflicts than are their children, who neither witness nor comprehend it all. Moreover, about seven in ten divorces today represent the termination of low-conflict marriages that, whatever their shortcomings, are generally better for children than divorce.[22] After comparing children of divorced couples with children of intact couples, Martin Seligman reported that he found

> a very nasty picture for the children of divorce. It used to be said that it is better for the children to have their unhappy parents divorce than to live with two parents who hate each other. But our findings show a bleak picture for these children: prolonged, unrelieved depression; a much higher rate of disruptive events; and, very strangely, much more apparently unrelated misfortune. It would be irresponsible for us not to advise you to take these dismaying data seriously if you are thinking about divorce.[23]

Seligman alludes to countless studies showing that, compared with children without two parents (and usually without involved fathers), children raised in stable two-parent homes are at decreased risk for poverty, school dropout, delinquency, emotional disorder, and substance abuse. (See appendix A, "Why Marriage Matters," for a consensus statement of social science findings.) The association between divorce and teen pathology "is a closer association than between smoking and cancer," observes University of Virginia researcher E. Mavis Hetherington.[24]

We need to be careful not to overstate the point: most kids in nontraditional families grow up healthy, and some kids in nurturing two-parent families struggle with depression, delinquency, and drugs. Still, the correlation between family structure and pathology occurs across families, across neighborhoods, and over time. Show us a place and time where nearly all children are co-parented by two adults who are enduringly committed to each other and their children, and we will show you a place and time with relatively low rates of poverty, disorder, and social pathology.[25] (This effect results *not* primarily from married parents shaping their children differently or having different values, but rather from healthier school, neighborhood, and peer influences that ride along with intact families.)[26]

Are children reared outside stable two-parent homes at risk because of their situation? Or are both family instability and child pathology common symptoms of some third factor, such as a stressed life in the economic underclass? "Children's well-being is more closely linked to parents' financial resources and stability than to marital status," argues the Alternatives to Marriage Project.[27] If kids from intact two-parent homes are half as likely to drop out of school as are children reared in one-parent homes, doesn't that merely reflect the greater poverty of unmarried parents?

Princeton sociologist (and former single mom) Sara McLanahan and University of Wisconsin sociologist Gary Sandefur respond:

> Children who grow up with only one parent are more likely to have problems in school, to drop out of school prematurely, to become teen mothers, and to have trouble finding a steady job, as compared with children who grow up with both parents. Parents . . . should realize that lack of income, and income loss associated with divorce, are responsible for about half of the disadvantages associated with living in a single-parent family, and that too little supervision and parental involvement and too much residential mobility account for most of the remaining disadvantage.

McLanahan and Sandefur also caution against thinking of poverty solely as a cause: "We view low income as partly the *result,* as well as partly the cause, of family disruption."[28] Divorce and nonmarital childbearing contribute to poverty. If you are concerned about poverty, the former Clinton policy adviser William Galston noted, you should want both a social safety net *and* a marriage-promoting culture: "The best anti-poverty program for children is a stable, intact family."[29] Marriage offers economies of partnership (with differing gifts contributed by each spouse and one less rent or mortgage payment), and it can provide both partners with a sense of responsibility and pride as stable, productive citizens. The columnist Molly Ivins put it baldly: "Economically, not to mention psychologically, becoming an unwed mother is a deeply dumb thing to do."[30]

Of course, if we statistically extract (or control for) the effects of factors such as income loss and dislocation, we can shrink the apparent effect of divorce or nonmarital childbearing. Similarly, if we extract the hurricane-associated wind, tidal surge, and flooding, we can shrink the apparent hurricane effect.[31] But neither makes sense, because family structure and hurricanes are both package variables.

One caveat: Some well-educated single professional women with adequate financial resources see themselves as exceptions to the rule. Yearning to become mothers, they became pregnant through artificial insemination when prospects for marriage dimmed and the biological clock kept ticking. Other mature single women have chosen to adopt. They are successfully raising children without spouses but with supportive networks of extended families and friends. Their situation is quite different from that of an unwed teenage mother living on the edge of poverty.

Even so, an important but little-known set of studies reveals that there's more to the family-structure effect than income loss. First, stepparent families have incomes similar to the incomes of originally intact families, but higher rates of child pathology. Consider, too, the National Center for Health Statistics's 1981 child-health survey of 15,416 randomly sampled children and its 1988 repeat of this survey with 17,110 more children.[32] The lead researcher, Nicholas Zill, recognized that intact and broken families differ in many ways: race, children's ages, parental education, income, and family size. So he statistically adjusted scores to extract such influences. In the first survey, those living with both parents were nonetheless *half* as likely as those living with a never or formerly married mother to have been suspended or expelled from school or to have had misbehavior reported by the school.[33] The follow-up survey confirmed these essential findings. Ergo, family breakup is not just a proxy for poverty.

But isn't what's toxic about family breakup more the preexisting marital conflict than the breakup per se? Consider another massive yet little-known study reported by a Johns Hopkins University team led by sociologist Andrew Cherlin. For thirty-three years at last report, researchers have followed over time most of the nearly eighteen thousand British children born during the first week of March 1958. For example, parents and teachers rated the behavior of nearly twelve thousand of these children as seven-year-olds and again four years later, knowing that in the intervening years some would have experienced divorce.[34] At the second rating, boys whose parents had divorced during the four years had more behavior problems than those whose families remained intact.

But we might wonder: are children's postdivorce problems influenced solely by the marriage breakup or also by the preexisting marital problems (divorce or no)? "Staying in an unhappy marriage is psychologically damaging," asserted another sociologist, Pepper Schwartz, "and staying only for the children's sake is ultimately not in your interest or anyone else's."[35]

So, rather than stay together for the sake of the children, should unhappy couples divorce for the sake of the children? The British researchers found that the problems experienced by children of divorce were less than halved by subtracting predivorce behavior differences between the two groups; predivorce misery did not fully explain the continuing increased rate of postdivorce problems.[36] In fact, when the researchers reinterviewed 12,537 of the participants at age twenty-three, controlling for predivorce family problems did *not* weaken the divorce effect. Yet another follow-up, this time with 11,759 of the participants at age thirty-three, confirmed the downward spiral of events that sometimes began with parental divorce.[37] By launching children into "negative life trajectories through adolescence into adulthood," the researchers concluded, divorce predicts increased social problems.[38]

Noting that family disruption doubles many risk factors for children, Nicholas Zill added that "in epidemiological terms, the doubling of a hazard is a substantial increase. . . . The increase in risk that dietary cholesterol poses for cardiovascular disease, for example, is far less than double."[39]

Is this case for marriage also a case against gay marriage?
Studies showing the benefits associated with stable co-parenting shed little direct light on an issue we will engage later: whether the benefits accrue only to mother-father co-parents and not to same-sex co-parents. "There have been more than 10,000 studies that have showed that children do best with a father and a mother," argued James Dobson in a 2004 webcast that rallied support for a federal marriage amendment that would ban gay marriages.[40] "In fact," he continued, "where children are raised with a committed mother and father the children are less likely to fail in school . . . be on drugs . . . be in poverty . . . commit suicide . . . get pregnant."

Dobson, as we've sought to demonstrate, is surely right about the benefits of marriage and co-parenting. It's better to have both a mother and a father than only a solo mother or father (or neither). That's important common ground that he shares with Hillary Clinton, that the Family Research Council shares with the Children's Defense Fund, and that the American Family Association shares with Planned Parenthood. "There is consensus," report researchers for the organization Child Trends, that unmarried teen childbearing "is undesirable—for the teen, for her baby, and for the larger society."[41] "Is it liberal or conservative," asks columnist Ellen Goodman, "to be worried about teenage mothers in the community?"[42]

But in terms of an argument against gay marriage, Dobson misstates the point. Most such studies compare children of intact married couples with single-parent children. Virtually none compare children of opposite-sex and same-sex couples. And virtually none compare children in single-parent or neglectful homes with children adopted or born into families where they are co-parented by two stable partners of the same sex. Will such children be harmed by not having a father (or a mother)? Or are two committed parents, regardless of gender, better than one? Stay tuned for more on this in chapter 9.

The Bottom Line

Marriage helps satisfy our need to belong. It predicts happy, healthy lives. And it forms part of a social ecology that nurtures flourishing children. Society—that's all of us—would benefit from the renewing of marriage. So, how might we create a more marriage- and child-supportive environment—a culture with neighborhoods filled with committed couples that take joy in the nurture of their flourishing children and with media and schools that support the values that all parents (single or married) tend to share? To that question we turn next.

Four

A Newer World

*Come, my friends,
'Tis not too late to seek a newer world.*
—Alfred, Lord Tennyson, "Ulysses"

STANDING ON THE BANK of a rushing river, a man spots a struggling woman being swept downstream. He heroically rescues her, administers first aid, and then spots another struggling person coming downriver and rescues him. After several more repetitions, the rescuer suddenly turns and starts running along the riverbank, ignoring yet another floundering person pleading for help. "Aren't you going to rescue that fellow?" asks a bystander. "No!" the rescuer shouts. "I'm going upstream to find what's pushing all these people in!"

We need support services that rescue and sustain struggling families. But we also need preventive medicine—upstream efforts to identify and reform the toxic social forces that knock people off life's riverbanks.

History teaches us that the way to reform the world is less by admonishing people ("Just say no") than by altering their environments. "Drive carefully" campaigns may have boosted safety a little, but divided highways and mandatory seat belts have accomplished more. Tolerance campaigns have changed our racial attitudes some, but desegregation has accomplished more. And consider how we've reduced our risk of fire deaths. Rather than just urging caution, our culture began requiring smoke detectors, sprinkler systems, and fire-resistant building materials. *Voilà!* Despite a 55 percent population increase since 1960, we've cut annual fire deaths in half.

Might we undertake comparable environmental changes that support marriages and families? Our marriages and our nurturing of flourishing, self-disciplined children are challenged by three toxic forces:

- the social consequences of unemployment and inequality
- media models of impulsive sexuality
- the increase in self-focused individualism

For each toxic force, there are responses that could strengthen our communal life without threatening important liberties. Here we explore responses to the first two social toxins. (In *The American Paradox: Spiritual Hunger in an Age of Plenty*, David explores the third, with suggestions on how to better balance a healthy "me" with a healthy "we.") If we can agree that marriage is generally good for adults (chapter 2), good for children (chapter 3), and good for society—because where marriage abounds, civility generally prevails and the social safety net requires fewer resources—then perhaps we people of faith can find some common ground in challenging toxic inequality, toxic media, and toxic individualism.

Home Economics

Poverty is sometimes demoralizing, often stressful, and usually limiting. Nevertheless, objective poverty per se is not the primary cause of family decline. Calcutta's families are more wretchedly poor than America's, yet more intact. In the first half of the twentieth century, African American families were mostly poor and mostly parented by married couples. And although families were in decline during the remainder of the century after 1960, a rising economic tide was lifting most boats and treating us to new pleasures. In 1960, only 15 percent of America's housing units enjoyed air-conditioning; when today's summers swelter, three out of every four of us manage to stay cool. "On sheer material grounds one would almost surely prefer to be poor today than upper middle class a century ago," observes economist Paul Krugman.[1] Today's working class enjoy luxuries—electricity, hot running water, flush toilets, television, and transportation—unknown to royalty of centuries past. Moreover, few of us would willingly return to the "good old days" of patriarchy, prejudice, and beehive hairdos.

Indeed, these are, in so many ways, the best of times. We are living longer, learning more, and making money like never before. New drugs shrink our tumors, manage our moods, and enlarge our potency. Women and various minorities enjoy formerly denied rights. Compared with a half century ago, we own twice as many cars per person, eat out two and a half times as often, pay much less (in real terms) for our milk and hamburgers, and enjoy our climate-controlled environments. Moreover, we *love* our e-mail, cell phones, TiVos, iPods, lattes, and Post-it notes. Not a bad life!

Inequality. But there is a problem. With executive salaries outpacing worker salaries, and with the richest fifth now earning as much as the other four-fifths, the yachts have risen faster and higher than the dinghies. Accompanying this growing economic inequality is growing economic segregation. Increasingly, the rich live separate from the poor, in enclaves with other rich, and their children attend well-funded suburban or private schools. Ironically, the welcome decrease in racial segregation has exacerbated this economic segregation. As educated, middle-class African Americans left Chicago's South Side after the 1950s, for example, they left behind an increasing concentration of joblessness, poverty, and fractured families.

Inequality is a mark of societies that have relatively few "very happy" people. (The egalitarian Scandinavians have been among the world's happiest folks.) Inequality also undermines marriage. A situation in which more young men have jobs with no future, or futures with no job, is likely to mean more young women with no husbands, more children without fathers in their lives, and more young men without the civilizing responsibilities of marriage and committed fatherhood. Show sociologist William Julius Wilson a place where joblessness runs high, and he will show you a place with an abundance of father-absent households.[2] When asked why Benton Harbor, Michigan, has so many single parents, retired mechanic Ken Parnell responded with exasperation, "Because black men can't get no jobs. . . . How can you take care of your family if you can't get a job?"[3]

Free markets and families. In his classic book *The Screwtape Letters,* C. S. Lewis imagined the thought processes of a senior devil named Screwtape, who devised ways in which humans could be tempted to choose wickedness over righteousness. Borrowing from Lewis, let's imagine that Screwtape wanted to design a plan to corrode marriage and the family. Might he not encourage corporate CEOs to act like yesteryear's robber barons and focus benefits on themselves while denying them to workers? Justifying corporate actions with talk of freedom, might he not coax them to deregulate television, legalize and spread gambling, structure taxes to penalize marriage, and shrink the real value of the minimum wage (which no longer would be a "living family wage" that protects families)? While sweeping more and more families downstream in a rushing demonic river, might Screwtape then advise the CEOs to beckon families to heroically swim upstream against the current; might he advise the CEOs to publicize the Horatio Alger–like examples of those who succeed against the odds, and to call those who drown "irresponsible"?

That may sound unappreciative of the many triumphs of the free-market economy. Yet even many conservatives now worry about unrestrained free markets harming families. The conservative spokesman William Bennett has called unbridled capitalism "a problem for that whole dimension of things we call the realm of values and human relationships."[4] In the conservative *Family in America* newsletter, Bryce Christensen worries that "Americans have witnessed nothing less than an assault upon wedlock and family life. We see this assault all around us: in heavy taxation of families with children; in the systematic dismantling of the family wage formerly making it possible to support a family on a single income."[5] George Will chides fellow conservatives who "see no connection between the cultural phenomena they deplore and the capitalist culture they promise to intensify."[6] The free market has given us Wi-Fi but also e-mail spam, strawberries in January but also global warming, cell phones but also the "splatter" video games played by the Columbine assassins. President Reagan's free-market deregulation of the media ("The marketplace will take care of children," said his FCC chair, Mark Fowler)[7] was followed by an immediate drop in educational programming, quality children's programming, and standards-and-practices oversight. Bennett, Christensen, and Will's wish is not for socialism but for a socially responsible capitalism—one that rewards initiative but also values healthy children and families (who will support the preservation of democracy and the free market).

Now imagine that Screwtape's angelic counterpart wanted to create an economic ecology that would instead enable stable, flourishing families. What would this utopian world look like? Might it be in some ways like our own, yet different? Might it offer

- full employment at livable wages as a higher priority;
- travel, restaurant, and store discounts not only to senior citizens (many of whom are increasingly affluent) but also to card-carrying custodial parents;
- inflation adjustments not only to senior citizens' Social Security payments but also to dependent exemptions and family assistance;
- tax policies that reward rather than penalize marriage;
- priority to married couples with children when allocating subsidized housing;
- corporate policies that minimize family uprootings; offer flex time, compressed time, and part-time work; welcome the home-based outsourcing of work; and equitably compensate workers and executives?

This much is certain: tax and corporate policies are also family policies. Families will benefit from a socially responsible capitalism that balances free-market competition with family supports. And family-supporting policies will, in the end, rebound to the benefit of business by supporting the civility and self-discipline that feed thriving enterprise. Conservatism, said the conservative writer Russell Kirk, cannot be "merely a defense of industrialism and industrial free market economics." It is, he adds, about "the cultivation and conservation of certain values, or it is nothing."[8]

Media and Minds

"The problem with television is that the people must sit and keep their eyes glued to a screen: The average American family hasn't time for it. Therefore the showmen are convinced that . . . television will never be a serious competitor of [radio]." So reported the *New York Times* in 1939. How wrong the showmen were. By the century's end, television was beaming its electromagnetic waves into children's eyeballs for more growing-up hours than they spend in school. Two-thirds of U.S. homes now have three or more sets, which helps explain why parents' reports of what their kids watch hardly correlate with their kids' reports of what they actually watch.[9]

"All of us who make motion pictures are teachers," the producer George Lucas has said, "teachers with very loud voices."[10] So, what is being taught? Here is a quick synopsis.

Does the reel world reflect the real world? Does Hollywood's world simply mirror the nasty real world? Content analyses reveal that television's world, with its few visibly old and few married people, isn't close to the real world.[11] Unlike the real world, where 87 percent of crimes are nonviolent, only 13 percent of prime-time crimes are nonviolent. Among some one hundred thousand violent acts the typical child views on television by the end of elementary school, 74 percent go unpunished and 58 percent show no victim pain.

Are sexual depictions truer to life? An average hour of network evening entertainment offers fifteen sexual acts, words, and innuendos. Nearly all involve unmarried partners, about half of which have no prior romantic relationship or have just met. And seldom does anyone communicate concern for birth control or sexually transmitted infection. In soap operas, unmarried partners have outnumbered married partners twenty-four to one. Moreover, in Hollywood's world (unlike the real world), women just love being forcibly taken: she resists, he persists, and before long the arms that were pushing him away are clutching him tight, her passions unleashed. (This "rape myth" message is hardly new. In *Gone with the Wind,* Scarlett O'Hara is carried to bed kicking and screaming and wakes up singing.)

When "they" (the young and unmarried) "do it" twenty thousand times a year on television and no one gets pregnant, herpes, or AIDS, that is massive sex *dis*information, says Planned Parenthood. And that's before considering the more intensive modeling of impulsive sexuality on music videos, cable movie channels, and millions of Internet XXX sites.

What does it matter? Does it matter if, instead of leaving our children to Beaver, we leave them to Beavis? Does prime-time crime influence our thinking and acting? Does on-screen sex shape our sexual expectations and behavior? Most teens and adults agree that there *is* an effect—on *other* people, "but not on me. . . . Don't worry, Mom. This stuff doesn't affect me." (Social psychologists call this others/not-me illusion the *third-person effect.*)

Everyone literate enough to be reading this book has heard about the hundreds of studies on the viewing of violence. Some studies correlate television viewing with thinking or behavior. Others experimentally manipulate viewing and note its effects. The consensus conclusions, affirmed in statements by the American Psychological Association,[12] the American Psychiatric Association,[13] the National Institutes of Mental Health, and other professional organizations can be summarized like this: Violence viewing

- *desensitizes people to cruelty.* An evil psychologist, note the researcher Edward Donnerstein and his colleagues, could hardly imagine a better way to make people indifferent to brutality than to expose them to a graded series of fights, killings, and slasher-movie mutilations.[14]
- *alters perceptions of reality.* To children and adults who view the world through television's screen, the world seems more menacing.
- *increases aggressive behavior.* When and where television was introduced, violent-crime rates jumped; in experiments, children randomly assigned to watch action programs often then imitate the witnessed kicks, punches, and shoves. (Recent experiments indicate that video-game violence is not only more graphic but also, thanks to the active role-playing, more socially toxic.)[15]

Less publicized but strikingly parallel results emerge from the viewing of what Hillary Clinton has called a "steady diet of impulsive sexuality."[16] As various studies have shown, such viewing

- *distorts perceptions of sexual reality.* When women's portrayed "No!" routinely dissolves to "Yes!" and when infidelity and impulsive sex are portrayed as everyday normality, viewers will tend to overestimate such behaviors (as teens routinely do when guessing their peers' behaviors, which in turn gives license for their own).
- *decreases attraction for comparatively less exciting partners.* Viewing perfect "10"s as they simulate passionate sex makes one's own partner seem more like a "6" than an "8"—and also makes people feel more dissatisfied with their own lumpy or spindly bodies.
- *primes men to perceive women in sexual terms.* After watching an erotic movie and later meeting a woman, men become much more likely to perceive and recall her physical features and to misinterpret her friendliness as a come-on.

- *makes sexual aggression seem less serious.* After repeated exposure to erotic fare, men become less judgmental of a rapist, and men and women become more accepting of extramarital sex, of women's sexual submission to men, and of men's seducing minors.
- *writes sexual "scripts."* Mental tapes—"social scripts"—automatically guide much of our behavior, so it's not surprising that saturation viewing of sexual innuendos and acts provides mental scripts for how to act in sexual situations.
- *increases sexual violence.* When and where pornography consumption has been high, sexual-violence rates have tended to be high as well. Experiments suggest that what's especially toxic is pornographic violence. "In laboratory studies measuring short-term effects," said a Surgeon General's consensus statement by twenty-one social scientists, "exposure to violent pornography increases punitive behavior toward women."[17]

Erotica that depicts impulsive sex may also be toxic. Social psychologist Neil Malamuth has identified two key ingredients of sexual aggression: "hostile masculinity" and "promiscuous-impersonal sex." If a steady diet of viewing sexual "hook-ups" distorts and primes sexual perceptions, makes sexual coercion seem more trivial, and provides accessible sexual scripts, then it surely makes a major contribution to the increase in "promiscuous-impersonal" sex.

It's Not Too Late to Seek a Newer World

Attributing any behavior, such as violence or risky sex, to a single cause is an oversimplification. Likewise, smoking is not cancer's only cause, but at the same time, the effects of smoking are not trivial. If media depictions of violence can desensitize and foster hostile perceptions and behaviors, that's also not trivial. And if saturation viewing of unrealistic sexual situations leads viewers to discount rape, devalue partners, and engage in uncommitted sex, that's not trivial, either.

Note that the point isn't about being puritanical (though many people prefer to keep their bodies and intimacies private). It isn't even about imposing a particular view of what's moral (though, as we've seen, eight in ten Republicans and eight in ten Democrats think "the overall state of moral values" is less than good, and in a 2004 postelection national survey, seven in ten Americans expressed concern that popular culture—television, movies, and music—is lowering moral standards).[18] Rather, it's strategic. You tell social scientists what sort of culture you'd like to live in, and they'll suggest a social blueprint for getting there. For example, would you like a world with low crime rates and without the economic and social costs of more than 2 million people (mostly young men) going to sleep behind bars each night? Would you like children nurtured in families and neighborhoods that increase the odds of their enjoying long and happy lives as mature, self-supporting adults who serve and enrich their communities? Would you welcome a much lower rate of child poverty? If so, you probably are also going to wish for tax laws, corporate policies, communal values, and media models that support covenantal relationships and stable co-parenting. On that much, "liberal" Marian Wright Edelman of the Children's Defense Fund and "conservative" James Dobson of Focus on the Family are pretty well agreed.

Morality aside, it then becomes strategic to expect media to offer social scripts of kindness, civility, attachment, and fidelity. If you *really* care about global warming, then you must also wish for fewer gas-guzzling SUVs and coal-fired power plants. Likewise, if you *really* care about advancing health and happiness and reducing juvenile crime and child poverty, then you've got to wish for a newer world—a social ecology that fosters stable, thriving families.

Reforming the media. The media's typical response has been to blame the mosquitoes: the problem, we're told, is parents who don't, hour by hour, monitor their children's media consumption. Parents should filter their children's viewing (which is rather like saying, "If you don't like the air pollution, don't breathe it; install air purifiers in your house"). "When Hollywood markets the worst and tells parents to do their best, it's like shooting holes in the family boat and telling us to keep plugging," notes Ellen Goodman.[19]

Recognizing that one cannot filter the media-influenced peer culture, the absorption of which is akin to breathing second-hand smoke, more and more parents would like to clean up the airwaves. Is this possible? Most Americans place greater priority on First Amendment freedoms than on Fourteenth Amendment equal protection for all (women and children included). We have, however, come to appreciate that sometimes social responsibilities trump individual rights. We accept open-housing laws that restrict our selling and renting in order to provide equal protection to all races. We accept restrictions on hate speech, private weaponry, leaf burning, smoking, unleashed dogs, parental irresponsibility, and drinking and driving—with laws that, as President Clinton's former domestic policy advisor William Galston has said, "convince citizens that the community is serious about its professed standards of responsibility."[20] In this spirit, should the United States follow the example of Canada, which limits media portrayals that demonstrably harm women (much as it limits proliferation of smelly garbage, polluting factories, and other things that harm the community)? As the aftermath of civil rights laws and court-ordered desegregation reminds us, we *can,* to some extent, legislate morality. Attitudes follow behavior.

Every country, including the United States, draws the line somewhere. "Censorship" is a red herring, because virtually everyone finds some materials, such as child pornography, as deserving of "restraint." But short of legal prior restraints, there is another policy option—to empower citizens to hold media legally responsible for their products' effects, just as citizens can hold drug or toy or tobacco companies responsible. If you produce and profit from a sexually violent video—an illustrated how-to manual on sexual abuse—then should someone who believes she was victimized by your product be free to try to prove a claim against you?

Awakening awareness. Our great need, however, is less for
censorship or litigation than for responsible citizenship. Prohibi-
tion failed because it was unsupported by the culture's moral
voice. Restraints on smoking in public places are succeeding
because health education has transformed public awareness.
Might public awareness similarly be roused about the media's
social and sexual scripts? For example, a recent study from the
Harvard School of Public Health has drawn attention to "ratings
creep," in which movies now rated PG and PG-13 show much
more sex, profanity, and violence than in the past. Professor Kimberly Thompson, the coauthor of the school's study of nearly two
thousand films from 1992 to 2003, said that "today's PG-13
movies are approaching what the R movies looked like in 1992"
and that "today's PG is approaching what PG-13 looked like a
decade ago."[21]

In the 1940s, movies often depicted African Americans as
childlike buffoons. Today, thanks to changed public consciousness,
such images, though not illegal, are unacceptable. In the 1960s
and 1970s, some rock music and movies glamorized drug use.
Responding to a tidal change in cultural attitudes, the entertainment industry began portraying the darker side of drug use, and
teen drug use then subsided.

As writers, producers, and actors became more health con-
scious, gratuitous movie smoking (picture Humphrey Bogart)
plummeted, and the number of smokers then dropped as well.
(Smoking in movies, which recently has undergone some resur-
gence, is tracked by the Web site SceneSmoking.org.)[22]

Responding to increased concern for animal rights, Hollywood
now voluntarily vouches for the humane treatment of animals in
films—and avoids depictions that degrade animals (nonhuman
animals, that is).

An informed and aroused public is a mighty force. "What
we're trying to do," explained feminist writer Gloria Steinem, "is
raise the level of awareness of violence against women and
pornography to at least the level of awareness of racist and Ku
Klux Klan literature."[23]

Here again there is broad agreement across the culture-war divide. No party or ideology has a corner on wishing for a culture of commitment. Thus liberal Democrat DeLores Tucker, chair of the National Congress of Black Women, could join conservative Republican William Bennett in challenging Time Warner executives on the lyrics of their gangsta rap recordings, which glorified rape, drugs, hatred of women and gays, and gruesome acts of murder. Are these profiteers "morally disabled?" Bennett later wondered aloud. (Following its well-publicized shaming, Time Warner divested itself of Interscope records, though not of the pornography channels on its cable systems).[24]

One needn't be liberal to agree with Steinem and Tucker, nor conservative to agree with Bennett. One needn't be anti-sex or pro-censorship to wonder whether we can't better balance liberty with responsibility. One needn't be anti-capitalist to observe that there is profit to be made in the collapse of civilization. One needn't wish for reruns of *Father Knows Best* to believe that sexual intimacy is most anxiety free and naturally satisfying when shared by a securely and permanently bonded couple. And one needn't devalue the Bill of Rights to hope that as we now shake our heads at yesterday's degrading racial images, so we may someday look back with embarrassment on the days when television, movies, and video games "entertained" people with scripts of sexual exploitation and human annihilation.

"Our utopian and perhaps naive hope," say media researchers Edward Donnerstein, Daniel Linz, and Steven Penrod, "is that in the end the truth revealed through good science will prevail and the public will be convinced that these images not only demean those portrayed but also those who view them."[25]

Fortunately, steps are now being taken to create this newer world:

- A slew of recent studies and books have made convincing cases for marriage and co-parenting. This information, summarized in chapter 3 and in this chapter, could now be integrated into high school health and sex-education curricula. (Given the misconceptions, it's needed: only one-third of America's high school seniors agree that most people are happier married, and 56 percent agree that having a child without being married is experimenting with a worthwhile lifestyle or not affecting anyone else.)[26]

- A bipartisan "marriage movement" has sprung up and has spun off marriage-promotion and mentoring initiatives in 150 communities. The Coalition for Marriage, Family and Couples Education, begun in 1996 to promote the spread of knowledge and skills to build satisfying marriages, drew nearly two thousand attendees to its recent annual meeting.[27]

- The National Marriage Project's *State of Our Unions* report, published annually since 1999, now provides the national media with research and analysis on trends in marriage.[28]

- With bipartisan support during the Clinton administration, character education has reentered the American educational agenda, aided by widespread agreement on core values such as trustworthiness, self-discipline, fairness, and kindness.

- "Abstinence Plus" sex-education programs are teaching both what liberals want (the benefits of safe sex) and what conservatives want (the benefits of saved sex). Again, the sex-war divide has been breached as more and more conservatives have begun to appreciate the wisdom of providing youth with realistic information about contraception, sexually transmitted infections, and condom-failure rates, and as more and more liberals have begun to appreciate the wisdom of educating youth about the satisfactions and life success that accompany a secure, lifelong partnership.

Thanks partly to these renewal efforts, teen intercourse, teen pregnancy, teen violence, and teen suicide have all abated since the early 1990s.

It is tempting to feel nostalgia for the good things of the past. Our task is to build a future that combines the good things we have lost with the good things we have gained, a future that affirms yesteryear's pair bonding and today's more egalitarian marriages, a future in which all sorts of parents in all sorts of families will find themselves riding not against the cultural winds, but with the winds at their backs.

Five

Understanding Sexual Orientation

Happy are those who find wisdom, and those who get understanding.
—Proverbs 3:13

SO FAR WE HAVE suggested dialoguing across the "great divide" in a spirit of humility. We have explained the human need to belong. We have indicated why marriage, and the decline of marriage, matters. And we have suggested routes to a marriage- and child-supporting culture.

Does the case for marriage extend to same-sex marriage? Before considering arguments for and against welcoming gay and lesbian people into marriage, let's consider what research has revealed about sexual orientation. What do most informed people of faith, whether "traditionalists" or "progressives," now agree upon? What's still at issue?

Note that we focus not on "homosexuality" but on *sexual orientation*. An analogy may help: People sometimes ask, "What causes left-handedness?" But that's not the scientific question. Rather, researchers compare right- and left-handed people in order to discern what influences *handedness* (everyone's). Thus, the scientifically more appropriate question is, why are most people right-handed and some people left-handed? What predicts this variation?

Likewise, researchers don't ask, "What causes homosexuality?" Instead they compare the anatomy, physiology, and experiences of straight and gay people in hopes of discerning what influences *sexual orientation.* Their studies shed as much light on heterosexuality as on homosexuality. Thus this chapter is about *everyone's* sexual orientation, ours and yours included.

Sexual orientation means an attraction toward members of either the other sex (heterosexual orientation) or one's own sex (homosexual orientation). Such attraction is revealed in our longings and fantasies. Those two categories, heterosexual and homosexual, will be our focus.

But isn't there a continuum of orientations, from exclusively heterosexual through bisexual to exclusively homosexual? Actually, although there is some variability, sexual orientation is one of the few human traits that are "bimodal" rather than distributed along a bell-shaped curve. Only about one in two hundred sexually active respondents in anonymous national surveys   12 out of 7076 Dutch adults in one recent survey,[1] 88 out of 14,460 American adults in National Opinion Research Center surveys[2]—report having both male and female partners in the last year. The percentage is only slightly higher if a longer reference period is taken into consideration.[3] These few people surely included some homosexual persons in heterosexual marriages. Thus the number of actively bisexual people—those who feel and enact sexual attraction to both sexes—appears minimal. With sexuality as with handedness, nearly everyone is disposed in one direction or the other, with few being genuinely ambidextrous. This is most clearly so with men. Women's sexuality, as we will see, varies more over time. Few people claim to be asexual (having "never felt sexually attracted to anyone at all")—only 1 percent, according to one recent large survey.[4] (A discussion of transgendered and intersexed persons is beyond our scope in this book.)

The Common Ground

Despite well-publicized and sometimes passionate disagreements about sexual orientation within the family of faith, there is also much agreement. Although differences always command attention, our conversation will be more civil if we remember that what unites us is deeper than what divides us. And we need to start with our faith.

The common ground in the basics of our faith. Today's followers of Jesus share a faith that God exists, loves us, and made this love manifest with a supreme redeeming act, which also serves as the supreme model for our own love for others. "Since God loved us so much, we also ought to love one another" (1 John 4:11). "No one has greater love than this, to lay down one's life for one's friends" (John 15:13). Whatever our differences, we agree that everyone is an image bearer of God, with immeasurable worth, and deserves respect. (Christians have therefore traveled the world in establishing hospitals and schools, knowing that compassion extended to even the least of those Jesus called his brothers and sisters is the same as compassion extended to him.) And whatever our disputes, we share a common hope—that death will not have the last word. In the end, the very end, offered the fourteenth-century mystic Dame Julian of Norwich, "all shall be well, and all shall be well, and all manner of things shall be well."

We also, as we noted in chapter 1, generally agree that truth is revealed through God's word (Scripture) and God's works (nature). Furthermore, we agree that pride is a deadly temptation, that we all are fallible and at times broken, and that we are called to worship God with an "ever reforming" spirit of humility. Finally, most of today's followers of Jesus agree that sexual fidelity and covenantal relationships are biblically supported and conducive to well-being. Thus we welcome marriage-supporting media and economic policies, and we celebrate the co-nurturing of children by adults who are committed to each other and to their children's welfare.

We Christians come in many varieties—mainline and evangelical, Pentecostal and Catholic, liberal and conservative. But on the big-ticket items we are discussing here, followers of Jesus pretty much agree. Whatever our differences, we stand on common ground.

The common ground in what we know about sexual orientation. Most of us not only agree on the basics of our faith but also have found some common ground in our emerging understanding of sexual orientation. We are likely to agree

- *on the numbers.* Homosexual orientation is not so common as the old "10 percent of people are gay" myth suggested. (As a general rule, distrust big round numbers offered without supporting data.) In surveys, with their privacy protected, something closer to 3 or 4 percent of men and 1 to 2 percent of women report being exclusively homosexual. In the National Opinion Research Center surveys, 97.5 percent of sexually active Americans report having only other-sex partners during the prior year. (Statistics tell us only the facts about something, not what to *do* about the facts. Whether left-handers are 3 percent or 10 percent of the population doesn't answer the question of whether left-handedness should be corrected or accepted.)
- *on compassion.* Acts of derision, harassment, intimidation, and violence toward anyone violate Christ's teaching. Our faith mandates love.
- *on the incompleteness of the science.* The causes of sexual orientation are just beginning to be understood. Because the scientific story is far from complete, any simplistic pronouncement ("Sexual orientation is programmed by our genes!") likely errs.
- *that science, rightly interpreted, has much to offer.* As people of faith in times past have allowed science to inform their understanding of the physical universe, so scientific findings may today inform our understanding of sexual orientation.
- *that science cannot, however, resolve values questions.* Even if science someday explains *why* people differ in sexual orientation, we will still have to decide whether to regard a homosexual orientation as a normal variation (as with left-handedness) or as an abnormality to be corrected (as with dyslexia). And whether straight or gay, we all face moral choices over options that include abstinence, fleeting "hook-ups," and long-term

commitment. As scientific explanation advances, moral responsibility does not recede.

Differences in How We View Sexual Orientation

Despite this considerable and growing common ground, differences remain. But by reaching across to one another in Christian love, we can view our differences as springboards for conversation rather than contention. Friends of kindred faith wrestle with their lingering differences on two key issues:

- *Should sexual orientation be regarded as a natural, given disposition or as a moral choice?* Is our sexual orientation something we're endowed with, by some combination of biological and environmental factors, or do our own choices also shape our sexual attractions? (The rest of this chapter engages this question.)
- *Can those wishing to change their sexual orientation undertake the effort with some reasonable hope of success?* Or are they better advised to "accept with serenity the thing that cannot be changed"? (The next chapter engages this question.)

One's answers to these two key questions, combined with one's biblical understanding, inform the Christian debate over two other big issues:

- *Are sexual intimacy and marriage for heterosexuals only?* Should gay and lesbian people refrain from expressing their sexuality even if in a committed relationship that is the social equivalent of marriage? Should the church advise celibacy for those not disposed to heterosexual marriage? Or is the satisfaction of our needs to belong and to share intimacy something for all humans to enjoy under a vow of commitment, faithfulness, and love?
- *How should the church respond to homosexual people?* Should monogamous, homosexual Christians be welcomed into church membership? Be invited to teach or sing in the choir? Be able to hold church offices? Be ordained?

Is Sexual Orientation a Choice or a Given Disposition?

"Homosexuality is a choice that people make, while race is something you cannot change," claims Rena Lindevaldsen, a lead attorney in the Liberty Counsel's efforts to challenge same-sex marriages.[5]

Others disagree. One lesbian Christian said that telling her she chose her sexual orientation is like telling her she chose the color of her eyes. "The color of my eyes is simply a natural part of me," she explained. "Oh, I could cover them up for a while, wear blue or brown contacts, but that wouldn't change the reality. My eyes are green, and my sexual orientation is gay."[6]

Is sexual orientation, as many believe, a moral or lifestyle choice? (Was your sexual orientation your choice?) Are heterosexuals those who've chosen wisely? Are homosexuals simply misbehaving heterosexuals?

The persistence of one's sexual attraction to either men or women suggests that sexual orientation is, for most if not for all, an enduring disposition. So, what determines our disposition?

Does Environment Influence Sexual Orientation?

Under Freud's influence, early explanations of sexual orientation assumed that childhood experiences bent the twig. To sleuth the twig-bending factors, researchers have asked questions such as these:

- Is homosexuality linked to problems in a child's relationships with parents, such as a boy's relationship with a domineering mother and an ineffectual father, or a possessive mother and a hostile father?
- Does homosexuality involve a fear or hatred of people of the other gender, leading individuals to direct their sexual desires toward members of their own sex?
- As children, were many homosexuals molested, seduced, or otherwise sexually victimized by an adult homosexual?

The answers appear to be no, no, and no. Consider, for example, the findings of lengthy Kinsey Institute interviews with nearly one thousand homosexuals and five hundred heterosexuals.[7] The investigators assessed nearly every imaginable influence on sexual orientation—parental relationships, childhood sexual experiences, peer relationships, dating experiences. Their findings: neither a close maternal relationship nor having a cold father explained the variation in sexual orientation.

And consider this: If "distant fathers" were more likely to produce homosexual sons, then shouldn't boys growing up in father-absent homes more often be gay? (They are not.) And shouldn't the rising number of such homes have led to a noticeable increase in the gay population? (It has not.)

Homosexual people do, however, appear more often in certain populations. For example, one study of the biographies of 1,004 eminent people found homosexual and bisexual people overrepresented (11 percent of the sample) especially among poets (24 percent), fiction writers (21 percent), and artists and musicians (15 percent).[8] In America's dozen largest cities, the percentage of men identifying themselves as gay jumps to 9 percent, compared with only 1 percent in rural areas.[9] (The 2000 U.S. Census found the highest percentage of same-sex unmarried partners in San Francisco, Miami, and Santa Fe.)[10] Probably, however, this reflects people's gravitating to agreeable vocations and cities rather than vocation and location affecting sexual orientation.

So, what does determine sexual orientation? One environmental theory proposes that people develop same-sex erotic attachments if segregated by gender at the time their sex drive matures.[11] Indeed, gay men tend to recall going through puberty somewhat earlier, when peers are more likely to be all male.[12] But even in a tribal culture in which homosexual behavior is expected of all boys before marriage, heterosexuality prevails.[13] (As this example illustrates, homosexual *behavior* does not always indicate a homosexual *orientation*.) Another environmental theory proposes the opposite: that people develop romantic attachments to those who *differ* from, and thus are more fascinating than, the peers they associate with while growing up. "The exotic becomes erotic."[14]

Environmental theories of sexual orientation continue to come and go, and one of these theories may someday find scientific support. For now, we can say that if there are environmental factors that influence sexual orientation, we do not yet know with any certainty what they are. Even today's more tolerant and accepting environment seems not to have altered rates of sexual orientation (despite fears about the influence of gay role models such as Ellen DeGeneres and Elton John). Nor has being reared in a straight, conservative home predetermined sexual orientation, as the gay or lesbian children of Vice President Dick Cheney, of the conservative activist Phyllis Schlafly, and of Pete Knight, a California state senator and the sponsor of California's anti-gay-marriage Proposition 22, could testify. Moreover, children reared by gay parents, like children reared by straight parents, usually grow up to be heterosexual. The bottom line: if someone were to ask us, "What can I do to influence my child's sexual orientation?" our answer would have to be "We haven't a clue."

Does Biology Influence Sexual Orientation?

As every psychology student knows, life experience and biology interact. A biological predisposition to obesity gets expressed in environments that offer abundant rich food with minimal energy expenditure. Biology plus environment equals obesity. Moreover, experiences leave footprints in our biology. Learning is written on the brain. Also, biological traits influence how our environment reacts to us. Studies indicate that homosexual men often were gender-nonconformist boys who had little interest in physical sports. This could have either an environmental or a biological explanation—or both. Perhaps, for example, a naturally less masculine-seeming child might be treated in ways that steer him toward homosexuality.

In general, though, environmental explanations of sexual orientation have receded and biological explanations have expanded.

"Evidence suggesting that biology plays an important role in the development of male and female sexual orientation is rapidly increasing," concluded psychologist Scott Hershberger after reviewing the available research.[15] Many other scientists agree with him. Data suggesting this conclusion are striking.

Same-sex attraction in animals. Two male penguins named Wendell and Cass at Coney Island's New York Aquarium are devoted, sexually active partners. So, too, are the Central Park Zoo penguins Silo and Roy. These and other "gay" penguins have much company in the wild kingdom. Nature is teeming with animals in which same-sex relations have, at least on occasion, been observed—more than 450 species, reports Bruce Bagemihl in *Biological Exuberance: Animal Homosexuality and Natural Diversity*.[16] The list includes grizzlies, gorillas, flamingos, owls, and even several species of salmon. In these animals, as in humans, opposite-sex contact is prevalent or the species would die out; but a minority exhibit same-sex attraction. Among rams, for example, some 6 to 10 percent— what breeding sheep ranchers call the "duds"—display same-sex attraction by shunning ewes and seeking to mount other males.[17]

Genes and sexual orientation. We can look for biological influences at three levels—genetic, neural, and biochemical (see Fig. 1). Our genes help organize our brains, which operate electrochemically. So, starting at the genetic level, can sexual orientation be passed on as part of heredity?

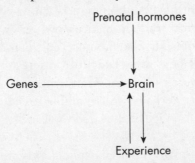

Fig. 1. Possible influences on sexual orientation

The available research does not, as yet, give a clear and consistent answer. There is, however, some tendency for sexual orientation to run in families.[18] "Studies indicate that male homosexuality is more likely to be transmitted from the mother's side of the family," reports a behavior-genetics team led by Robert Plomin.[19]

Because family members share environments as well as genes, scientists prefer to examine genetic factors by comparing fraternal twins (who typically share environments) with identical twins (who also are genetic clones). A pair of early 1990s studies conducted by Northwestern University psychologist Michael Bailey and his colleagues looked at the twin siblings of homosexual men and women.[20] Their finding: compared with fraternal twins, identical twins were more than doubly likely to share a homosexual orientation.

Because many identical twins have differing sexual orientation, we know that genes aren't the whole story. Moreover, new studies using more diverse samples of Australian and American twins have found somewhat lower rates of sexual similarity— although, again, identical twins were more likely than fraternal twins to share homosexual feelings.[21] This is the sort of pattern we expect to see when genes are having some influence but other factors are, too.

The search for an X-chromosome-linked "gay gene" also has yielded mixed results. With a single transplanted gene, scientists have caused male fruit flies to display homosexual behavior.[22] With humans, one well-publicized apparent discovery of a gay gene has not been consistently replicated, leaving the finding in doubt. One National Institutes of Health–funded five-year study of the genetics of male homosexuality, conducted by Alan R. Sanders and begun in the fall of 2003, will analyze blood samples from some one thousand pairs of homosexual brothers.[23] In time, we likely will know more.

The very idea of genetic influences on sexual orientation is puzzling. Just as people ask, "Why do men have nipples?" so people ask why "gay genes," had they ever existed, would not have disappeared from the human gene pool (given that same-sex partners cannot reproduce). Researchers offer several possible answers:

- *Kin reproductive success.* One theory reminds us that many of our genes also reside in our kin. Perhaps, then, gay people's genes lived on through the survival and reproductive success of their relatives (who also carry many of those genes.)
- *A composite of adaptive traits.* Another theory speculates that different genes predispose different adaptive traits that, in combination, may result in homosexuality. Different genes, for example, may predispose attractive male traits such as sensitivity, empathy, and kindness. When the genetic lottery brings these all together, perhaps, in combination with unusual hormone levels in the womb, homosexuality may be the natural result.
- *The mother's successful genetics.* A recent Italian study confirms what others have found—that homosexual men have more homosexual relatives among their maternal than their paternal relatives. The data also showed that maternal relatives of homosexual men produce more offspring than those of heterosexuals.[24] Perhaps, surmised the researchers, genes that predispose a reproductive advantage in mothers and aunts can influence sexual orientation in their sons and nephews.

The brain and sexual orientation. Neuroscientists have uncovered some brain structures that appear linked to sexual orientation. Simon LeVay discovered one such structure while studying sections of the hypothalamus taken from deceased heterosexual and homosexual people.[25] As a gay scientist, LeVay wanted to do "something connected with my gay identity." He knew he had to avoid biasing the results, so he did the study "blind," without knowing which donors were gay. For nine months he peered through his microscope at a cell cluster known to be involved in sexuality. Then one morning, he sat down and broke the codes. His discovery: the cell cluster was reliably larger in heterosexual men than in women and homosexual men. As the brain difference became apparent, "I was almost in a state of shock. . . . I took a walk by myself on the cliffs over the ocean. I sat for half an hour just thinking what this might mean."[26]

Given that everything psychological is also biological (we are embodied beings), it should not surprise us that brains differ with sexual orientation. The critical question is, when did the brain difference begin? At conception? In the womb? During childhood or adolescence? Did experience produce the difference? Or was it genes or prenatal hormones (or genes via prenatal hormones)?

LeVay does not view this neural center as a center for sexual orientation; rather, he sees it as an important part of the neural pathway engaged in sexual behavior. He acknowledges that sexual behavior patterns influence the brain's anatomy. In fish, birds, rats, and humans, brain structures vary with experience—including sexual experience, reports sex researcher Marc Breedlove.[27] So maybe, said skeptics, the sexual history, or the AIDS illness that claimed many of these lives, explained the difference. But LeVay believes that in this case it's more likely that brain anatomy influences sexual orientation. "Gay men simply don't have the brain cells to be attracted to women," he conjectured.[28] His hunch recently was confirmed by the discovery of a similar hypothalamic difference between the 6 to 10 percent of rams that display same-sex attraction and the 90-plus percent attracted to females.[29] Moreover, University of London psychologists Qazi Rahman and Glenn Wilson report that "the neuroanatomical correlates of male homosexuality differentiate very early postnatally, if not prenatally."[30]

Neuroscientists Laura Allen and Roger Gorski have independently concluded that another part of brain anatomy also predicts sexual orientation. Their discovery, which awaits replication, is that a section of the anterior commissure (fibers connecting right and left hemispheres) is one-third larger in homosexual men than in heterosexual men.[31] All in all, concluded Brian Gladue in a research synopsis, "the emerging neuroanatomical picture is that, in some brain areas, homosexual men are more likely to have female-typical neuroanatomy than are heterosexual men."[32]

Prenatal hormones and sexual orientation. Hormone levels in adults give us no clue to people's sexual orientation. But prenatal hormone exposure does. In animals and some exceptional human cases, sexual orientation has been altered by abnormal prenatal hormone conditions. The German researcher Gunter Dorner pioneered this research by manipulating a fetal rat's exposure to male hormones, thereby "inverting" its sexual behavior toward rats of the other sex.[33] Feminized male rats (male rats deprived of prenatal testosterone) will raise their rump, inviting other male rats to mount them; masculinized female rats (female rats exposed to excess prenatal testosterone) will mount other females. Female sheep will likewise show homosexual behavior if their pregnant mothers are injected with testosterone during a critical gestation period.[34]

With humans, a critical period for the brain's neural-hormonal control system may exist between the middle of the second month and the fifth month after conception.[35] Exposure to the hormone levels typically experienced by female fetuses during this time appears to predispose the person (whether female or male) to be attracted to males in later life.

Prenatal influences may also help account for some other curious findings:

- *Male birth order.* Men who have older brothers are somewhat more likely to be gay, report Canadian psychologists Ray Blanchard and Anthony Bogaert.[36] Assuming that the odds of homosexuality are roughly 3 percent among first sons, they rise to about 4 percent among second sons, 5 percent among third sons, and so on for each additional older brother. The reason for this phenomenon—what researchers call the *fraternal birth-order effect*—is unclear. Blanchard suspects a defensive maternal immune response to foreign substances produced by male fetuses. The maternal antibodies may become stronger after each pregnancy with a male fetus and may prevent the fetus's brain from developing in a male-typical pattern. Women with older sisters, and women who were womb mates of twin brothers, exhibit no such sibling effect.[37]

- *Fingerprint patterns.* Curiously, in some (but not all) studies, gay men have had fingerprint patterns rather like those of heterosexual women.[38] Most people have more fingerprint ridges on their right hand than on their left. Jeff Hall and Doreen Kimura first observed that this difference was greater for heterosexual males than for females and gay males.[39] Given that fingerprint ridges are complete by the sixteenth fetal week, the researchers suspected that the difference was due to prenatal hormones.

- *Handedness.* Prenatal hormones also are a possible explanation for why data from twenty studies revealed that "homosexual participants had 39 percent greater odds of being non-right-handed."[40]

- *Hearing.* Lesbians may likewise have more male-typical anatomy. In one study, the cochlea and hearing system of lesbians had developed in a way that was intermediate between those typical of heterosexual females and those typical of heterosexual males, a difference that seemed attributable to prenatal hormonal influence.[41]

- *Spatial ability.* One of the few consistent and fairly substantial gender differences is males' greater average spatial abilities, as illustrated in their scores on mental rotation tasks such as the task illustrated in figure 2. (Which of the four figures could be rotated to match the target figure at the top?) A study by Qazi Rahman and colleagues with an ample sample of heterosexual and homosexual males and females illustrates the common finding that homosexual persons (both male and female) score *between* heterosexual males and females.[42]

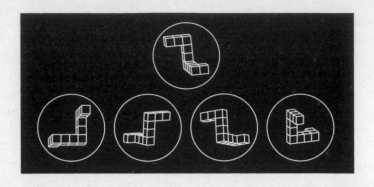

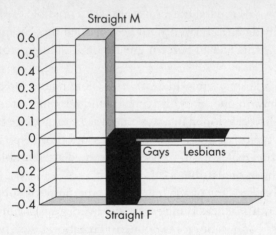

Fig. 2. Mental rotation scores, by sexual orientation (Z-scores from Qazi Rahman, Glenn Wilson, and Sharon Abrahams, "Biosocial Factors, Sexual Orientation and Neurocognitive Functioning," Psychoneuroendocrinology *29 [2004]: 867–81. Sixty people per group.)*

Conclusions

Accumulating evidence points to brain differences and prenatal hormonal influences as helping to explain sexual orientation. Studies have also found that heterosexual and homosexual individuals vary in other ways unlikely to have been influenced by upbringing or choice, including fingerprint patterns and spatial abilities, and also physical size (gay men tend to weigh less), and even subtle differences in relative finger lengths, female eye-blink patterns, and length of sleep (one study found gays and lesbians sleeping somewhat less, and other research has found a brain difference that could account for such a difference).[43] The tendency of homosexual individuals of both sexes to fall between heterosexual females and males crosses many of these traits.

Some of these findings are preliminary, and some may be disconfirmed by further research. Even so, the table of evidence has an increasing number of legs underneath, legs supporting the conclusion that sexual orientation is naturally predisposed. Virtually all of us agree that this conclusion also finds support in our own experience. We didn't choose our fantasies and longings directed toward persons of our own sex or persons of the other sex. Like Web-site pop-up ads, they just started appearing. The key is arousal, not behavior.

Two cautionary notes: First, women's sexual orientation has been less often studied (there are more gay men than lesbians) and is, as one recent scientific review put it, "poorly understood."[44] Women's sexual orientation also tends to be less strongly felt and potentially more fluid and changeable than men's, note psychologists Lisa Diamond, Anne Peplau, and Linda Garnets.[45] Men's lesser sexual variability is apparent in this and many other ways as well, notes social psychologist Roy Baumeister.[46] Across time, across cultures, and across situations, women's sexual drive and interests are more flexible and varying than men's—a phenomenon Baumeister calls the gender difference in "erotic plasticity." Diamond writes that some of the recent questioning and reconceptualization of women's sexuality "does not deny potential biological contributions to women's same-gender sexual desires" but grants them less weight.[47]

Second, we as yet glimpse only in a dim mirror the precise ways in which biology and experience interact. Rather than specifying sexual orientation, perhaps biological factors predispose a temperament that influences sexuality in the context of experience.

Perhaps, theorizes Cornell psychologist Daryl Bem, genes carry a code for prenatal hormones and brain anatomy, which predispose temperaments that lead children to prefer gender-typical or gender-atypical activities and friends, which preference then directs their sexual orientation.[48] If experience does play a role in programming sexual orientation, it's just an alternate method for shaping the brain. (Nature and nurture both make deposits in the brain, notes neuroscientist Joseph LeDoux, much as you get the same result whether wiring money into your bank account or handing cash to a teller).[49]

Regardless of the process, the consistency of the genetic, neural, and biochemical findings has swung the pendulum toward a greater appreciation of biological influences. If biology indeed proves critical (perhaps especially so in certain environments), such would explain why we do not experience our own sexual orientation as a choice.

But is it subject to change? To that we turn next.

Six

Changing Sexual Orientation

O God, give us grace to accept with serenity the things that cannot be changed,
courage to change the things which should be changed, and the
wisdom to distinguish the one from the other.
—Reinhold Niebuhr, "The Serenity Prayer"

AN AFFIRMATIVE ANSWER to Reinhold Niebuhr's famous prayer begins with the wisdom to distinguish what we can change from what we cannot. Some traits, it's now clear, are naturally predisposed and not amenable to change; other characteristics lie within our control.

Our temperament is one trait that we receive rather than choose. From womb to tomb, some people tend to be excitable, intense, and reactive; others are easygoing, quiet, and placid. People may mellow a bit with age, but the hot-tempered young adult usually becomes the relatively irascible older person. That being so, we had best find the serenity to accept and wisely manage our temperament—and try to understand the temperaments of those around us.

Our body type is also naturally predisposed. People used to presume that obesity resulted from gluttony, from a failure of the will, or from repressed guilt or hostility. With effort or therapy one presumably could elect a different body. But the truth is told by studies of identical twins (who share similar body types) and of adopted children (who resemble their biological parents more than their adoptive parents and siblings). Although diet and exercise can make a difference, our body fights to maintain its "settling point" weight, much as a thermostat maintains room temperature at a set point.

Other things we *can* change. In *What You Can Change and What You Can't*, clinical researcher Martin Seligman offers facts about what you can change:

> The sexual "dysfunctions"—frigidity, impotence, premature ejaculation—can be unlearned.
> Our moods, which can wreak havoc with our physical health, can be controlled.
> Depression can be alleviated by changes in conscious thinking or helped by medication, but rarely alleviated or helped by insight into childhood.
> Optimism is a learned skill. Once learned, it increases achievement at work and improves physical health.[1]

What about sexual orientation? Even if we didn't willfully choose it and our parents didn't shape it, can we change it?

On the assumption that what has been learned can be relearned differently, conservatives have tended to favor environmental explanations of sexual orientation. Their belief that sexual orientation is chosen makes it easier for them to go to the next step and argue that gays and lesbians can make a new choice for heterosexuality, leaving their former, homosexual lives behind. Conversely, liberals (and gays) have tended to welcome biological explanations on the assumption that what's biologically disposed should be accepted: "We know from our own experience that sexual orientation is inborn, and can't be changed," explains gay blogger Scott Bidstrup.[2]

Actually, some learned behaviors are enduring. (Examples range from human language accents to ducklings imprinted to follow whatever they were exposed to at their life's beginning— usually their own mother, but sometimes a merry prankster researcher.) And some biological traits are modifiable or controllable. (Examples range from vision correction with glasses to growth hormones that correct dwarfism.) Thus understanding the *roots* of sexual orientation doesn't settle the question of whether sexual orientation can change.

On this question, there's a big divide among people of faith. A 2003 Pew Research Center study reported that, by a four-to-one margin, "highly committed" evangelicals who expressed an opinion believe that sexual orientation *can* be changed. By a two-to-one margin, mainline Protestants (and white Catholics by a similar margin) think it *can't*.[3] Nevertheless, those on both sides of this debate agree on some things.

Possible Areas of Agreement

First, people can act against their desires. Heterosexual prisoners may engage in sex with cell mates. Homosexuals can fulfill others' expectations by marrying and having children. (Genital friction, sometimes combined with eyes-closed fantasies, can produce intended results.) Sexual orientation is what one is, not what one does.

Second, sexual orientation is not reversed by experimentation. Heterosexuals (for whom opposite-sex attractions feel natural) may experiment with homosexual behavior, and homosexuals (for whom same-sex attractions feel natural) may experiment with heterosexual behavior, but both readily turn away from such. The handedness analogy is applicable here. Using the right hand feels natural to right-handed people. Using the left hand feels natural to left-handed people. Persons in either category might try using the other hand for certain tasks (say, holding a fork or writing), but that does not mean they've switched their basic handedness, and they quickly turn back to what is natural for them.

Third, people of either sexual orientation can struggle to resist enacting their desires or even to live a celibate life.

Fourth, doing so isn't easy (and sexually active married people might therefore think twice about preaching what they themselves don't practice, lest they replicate the Pharisees of whom Jesus said, "They tie onto people's backs loads that are heavy and hard to carry").[4] *Christianity Today* offered the testimony of one married gay man who reported that with prayer, counseling, and great effort he was able to "control the behavioral manifestations of my sexual orientation" and to have a "fulfilling heterosexual life" even while struggling with his continuing attractions to other men and his "recurring bouts of almost suicidal depression."

Reparative Therapy

In decades past, mental health workers sought to change sexual orientation with treatments ranging from psychoanalysis to aversion therapy (which, for gay males, meant pairing electric shocks with pictures of naked men). Such methods were largely ineffective and therefore abandoned. Then in the 1980s, British theologian-turned-psychologist Elizabeth Moberly and, soon after, American psychologist Joseph Nicolosi followed Freud's lead in suggesting that early parent-child relationships shape the sexual clay.[5] They have argued that a young boy, suffering a painful mismatch between his needs and what his disappointing father offers, may "defensively detach" from his father. Still longing for the warmth and love his father never gave him, he may develop attachments to older boys who help fill that vacuum. After puberty, such longing for male intimacy supposedly becomes sexualized.

"I looked at all of my gay male friends," explains Mike Haley of Focus on the Family's Love Won Out gay minstry, "and there was incredible familial trouble, strife, difficulty; there were no happy upbringings. . . . There was no 'click' with the father."[6]

In keeping with Freudian psychology's history of parent blaming, the implication for dads seems clear: If they are distressed to find themselves with a gay son, they've got themselves to blame. Homosexuality is said to be their son's effort to repair the broken or nonexistent father-son relationship, and during therapy their sons may learn to voice how distant or unnurturing their dads were.

Reparative therapy (sometimes called *conversion therapy* or *reori-*

entation therapy) seeks to redirect the repair effort by offering the gay client intimate nonsexual relationships with other males via the therapist and peers in support groups. Men are encouraged to develop their sense of masculinity (and women their femininity) on the assumption that strong gender identifications promote heterosexuality. Because the therapy espouses sexual reorientation and teaches traditional gender roles, conservative Christian groups (which normally would steer clear of Freudian ideas) have promoted reparative therapy.

The major American mental health associations, representing nearly half a million professionals, are essentially unanimous in rejecting the basic assumption of reparative therapy—that homosexuality is a disorder that needs a cure—and in challenging the belief that such therapy can enable gay men and lesbians to reverse their sexual desires. Several of the associations have declared (displaying their politically correct biases, say critics) that reparative therapy has potential for harm. Some sample statements:

American Psychological Association: "Can therapy change sexual orientation? No. . . . The reality is that homosexuality is not an illness. It does not require treatment and is not changeable."[7]

American Academy of Pediatrics: "Therapy directed specifically at changing sexual orientation is contraindicated, since it can provoke guilt and anxiety while having little or no potential for achieving changes in orientation."[8]

National Association of Social Workers: "Sexual orientation conversion therapies assume that homosexual orientation is both pathological and freely chosen. No data demonstrate that reparative or conversion therapies are effective, and in fact they may be harmful."[9]

American Psychiatric Association: "The potential risks of 'reparative therapy' are great, including depression, anxiety and self-destructive behavior, since therapist alignment with societal prejudices against homosexuality may reinforce self-hatred already experienced by the patient." Some persons seek out reparative therapy after being "inaccurately told that homosexuals are lonely, unhappy individuals who never achieve acceptance or satisfaction."[10]

The assertion that *gay* is a misnomer and can't possibly mean "happy" is made frequently by those promoting change. Writer Tim LaHaye (known for his popular "Left Behind" fiction series) entitled a 1978 book of his *The Unhappy Gays*.[11] More recently, Erwin Lutzer, while urging compassion, asserts, "No matter what we see on television, the gay community is hurting, compulsively acting out behavior to cover their pain."[12] Helping gays and lesbians change is thus viewed as an act of kindness toward them, a way of steering them toward a happier life. This belief, along with a belief that homosexuality is contrary to God's will, has spawned religious organizations devoted to helping gay men and lesbians move out of homosexuality.

Ex-Gay Ministries

"Change is possible," declares the home page of Exodus International, a network of 135 ministries to homosexual persons in seventeen nations. It goes on to say that Exodus proclaims "the Biblical truth that freedom from homosexuality is possible when Jesus is Lord of one's life. . . . Exodus affirms reorientation of same sex attraction is possible."[13]

Hearing such claims, and hoping to find relief from their struggles, Christian homosexuals may turn to such "transformational ministries." Many have been rejected by their families and churches. They have prayed repeatedly—often for many years— that God will deliver them from their same-sex desires. They have gone forward in revival services, talked with ministers, made promises to God. Some have sought change through therapy, entered marriages to persons of the other sex, even tried exorcism. Some have asked God to let them die or have actually attempted suicide. Groups that promise them escape from their homosexual proclivities seem to be the answer they have been looking for.

Arguing that "homosexuality is preventable and treatable," Mike Haley, chair of the Exodus board of directors and manager of Focus on the Family's "homosexuality and gender department," offers his own testimony: "I went from having homosexual fantasies and dreams, and feeling that a sexual relationship with a woman was repulsive, to the opposite end of the spectrum of having a sexually gratifying, emotionally satisfying relationship with my wife. . . . I prove homosexuality is not immutable, that it can be changed."[14]

What troubles skeptics is that time and again such powerful testimonials turn out to have been false, self-deceptive, or from people who never were genuinely homosexual. More than a dozen such organizations have, after touting successes, been abandoned by their own founders, who are now *ex*-ex-gays." Jeff Ford, a former executive director of a Minnesota ex-gay program and a former "national speaker for Exodus," acknowledges that, despite his claims of being "healed" of homosexuality and of helping others to be "healed," he actually "did not see that happen in my work with over three hundred gay and lesbian people."[15]

In Britain, the formerly ex-gay organization Courage Trust is no longer attempting sexual reorientation. Its founder, Jeremy Marks, explained that his organization "not only failed to preserve the moral purity of gay people (or the church) but, on the contrary, has proved to have an extremely destructive effect on the lives of many gay people [and] has had an extremely corrosive effect on their faith in God."[16] According to the organization's Web site:

> During the early 1990s, Courage ran a succession of discipleship programmes with a view to helping people "come out" of homosexuality. However, practical experience proved this to be a counter-productive approach. Through our years of pastoral experience, it became increasingly imperative to listen to the Holy Spirit afresh and pursue further scriptural study on the issues. The result is that we have come to recognise that God supports and blesses sincere committed relationships

between gay people (for whom a heterosexual relationship is inappropriate).

Today, Courage Trust declares itself "an evangelical Christian organization [for] gay and lesbian Christians who are seeking a safe place of friendship in which to reconcile their faith and sexuality and grow towards Christian maturity."[17]

Clint Trout, now with the AIDS Healthcare Foundation, illustrates the earnestness with which some people seek reorientation:

Confident and determined to become heterosexual, I began my five years of reparative therapy. My counselor acquainted me with Exodus International. . . . The cornerstone of their psychotherapy is the theory that people are gay because of a breakdown in the relationship with their same-sex parent. . . .

My life was centered on becoming straight. I went to therapy twice a week and group once a week. I read approximately 50 books on the subject. I attended about five conferences on reparative therapy. I had hundreds upon hundreds of prayer sessions, some of which lasted all night. I confessed every fantasy and experience of attraction. I was bathed in holy water and holy oil. I was baptized twice.

[Four and a half years later] I was still gay. Though I had never even kissed a man, my longing for both emotional and physical intimacy with one was almost overpowering. Despite all of the prayer, confession and therapy, nothing changed that fact. . . .

Of the several hundred people in "ex-gay" ministries I have met, at conferences, groups, and my own fledgling ministry, I never met anyone who had overcome his or her desire to be with people of the same sex.[18]

The ex-gay-ministry literature acknowledges the continued struggles with homosexual temptations experienced by many who consider themselves no longer gay. "God does not replace one form of lust with another," explained Bob Davies and Lori

Rentzel in *Coming Out of Homosexuality*. Ex-gays commonly are aware of homosexual attraction and typically "do not experience sexual arousal solely by looking at their wife's body." According to Davies, "*ex*-ex-gays" are people who "abandon their previously-held view that homosexual behavior is sin . . . [and] go with their feelings, rather than submit to the author of the Scriptures."[19]

Consistent with such candid statements from the leading ex-gay ministry, gay evangelical psychotherapist Ralph Blair observes that "when pressed, and in fine print, what reparative therapy and the ex-gay movement admit is that people are trying to control the expression of their sexual urges. (And some who are helped to do so are coming from extremely sordid sexual lifestyles.) There are a few claims of reorientation but these are becoming fewer and fewer. And those that have claimed reorientation keep 'falling.'"[20]

Consider statements from the Exodus organization after the ex-gay leader John Paulk—Mike Haley's predecessor as chair of the Exodus board of directors, the head of Focus on the Family's transformation ministry to homosexuals, and a featured ex-gay on the cover of *Newsweek*—was found in a gay bar. Exodus staff director Davies stated that "as an organization, we also need to re-examine . . . the public perception of our use of terms such as 'healing' and 'change.'"[21]

Shortly before this embarrassing incident, Exodus was faced with the publicity of another ex-gay who recanted his testimony of therapy- and prayer-aided sexual transformation, saying "his sexual orientation had not in fact changed, that he is and always has been a homosexual, and that he does not believe that ex-gay ministries can ever change an individual's sexual orientation."[22] Such mere anecdotes are not, by themselves, especially informative. What's more interesting is the Exodus press release in response to it:

> "Reading these stories [of people who have returned to their homosexual identity] is certainly heartbreaking," said Bob Davies, North American director of Exodus International. "But I find it interesting that the entire focus of each individual

seemed to be changing their sexual orientation. That was very different from my focus upon entering Exodus many years ago." Davies said that he came to Exodus for support in living out his Christian convictions that homosexual behavior was sinful.[23]

Is there a bridge across the divide here? To the extent that "healing" ministries aim not, as they publicly declare, to reverse sexual *orientation* but to support people in escaping unrewarding and unhealthy sexual *behaviors,* and in living free of drugs and alcohol, most people of faith could applaud their efforts. (Regardless of one's sexual orientation, there *are* moral and health-related issues worth contemplating.) Transformational-ministry advocates and skeptics agree that sexual *behavior* can change; some people can be convinced to choose celibacy, and others to marry someone of the other sex (even if that often involves fantasizing about a same-sex person during lovemaking). Advocates and skeptics also agree that sexual *identity* can change, as ex-gay support groups encourage members to think of and proclaim themselves as no longer gay (unlike AA members, who view themselves as forever alcoholic and vulnerable to relapse).

Virtually everyone further agrees that sexual *orientation* is more resistant to change. Reparative therapists and ex-gay ministries nevertheless declare that in many cases it can change; the mental health associations are skeptical. Thus the issue narrows to whether, aided by therapy and ministry, the *likelihood* of sexual reorientation is sufficient to encourage the effort, rather than encouraging people "to accept the thing that cannot be changed." Is the failure rate of reparative therapy and ex-gay transformation ministries 70 percent? 90 percent? 100 percent? And if the failures bear a cost of increased guilt, depression, and risk of suicide, what success level would warrant encouraging those desiring change to enter such therapy?

At the same time, Christians must be cautious about invalidating any individual's personal experience. Only the person and God know what the true "before" and "after" have been—and why. As an article on ChristianLesbians.com, an Internet site that supports Christian lesbians and supports lesbian couples in their relationships and faith, acknowledges,

> I believe it's vitally important that none of us, whether lesbian or "ex-lesbian" discredit the work of God in someone else's life simply because it seems to conflict with our own experience. . . . To me, the miracle in each of these stories isn't that a woman no longer has same-sex affections and relationships but that each was healed from unforgiveness, bitterness, painful memories, anger, and self-hatred. They have grown in their understanding that God loves them, in the knowledge of their total dependence on God in all things, and in their desire to submit all of their life to God's control. These are the same things I celebrate in the lives of many Christian lesbians. We might possibly have more in common than we dare to imagine.[24]

The article lists experiences common among women who claim healing from deep emotional pain through an ex-gay ministry. The lives these women have left behind, and the issues they have dealt with, run far deeper than same-sex sexual involvement. The article points out, however, that affirming such personal stories doesn't negate the fact that many *other* women and men have left ex-gay movements emotionally wounded or disillusioned rather than helped.

Convincing Evidence of Change?

The battle of anecdotes of supposed sexual reorientation versus anecdotes of failures and of ex-ex-gays will not resolve the issue. Just as we don't trust anecdotal before-and-after diet-ad photos as a substitute for evidence, so we should be cautious about drawing conclusions from anecdotes of sexual-reorientation successes and failures. What's needed is some decisive evidence.

For many sexual-reorientation proponents, persuasive evidence seemed to come at the 2001 American Psychiatric Association convention, when Robert Spitzer presented a report titled "200

Subjects Who Claim to Have Changed Their Sexual Orientation from Homosexual to Heterosexual." "Psychiatrist Now Says Homosexuals Can Change," headlined the American Family Association.[25] "Robert Spitzer's recent study argues that people can change their homosexual behavior," echoed *Christianity Today*.[26] The study became prominent national news partly because its author was a Columbia University psychiatrist who nearly three decades earlier had played a key role in getting homosexuality eliminated from the psychiatric classification of disorders.[27] After talking with several self-proclaimed ex-gays at the 1999 American Psychiatric Association meeting, Spitzer got to wondering about their claims. Hoping to satisfy his curiosity, he found, with assistance from ex-gay ministries and the reparative therapy association (NARTH)—though "with great difficulty"—274 Americans who called his office hoping to provide their evidence of change.[28]

With hundreds of therapists belonging to the reparative therapy association, each presumably with many present and past clients, and with more than 120 Exodus-affiliated organizations with numerous members, one might have presumed a willing pool of tens of thousands of ex-gays. In fact, reports Spitzer, "it was necessary to repeatedly send notices of the study over a 15-month period to a large number of participants who had undergone some form of reparative therapy" in order to recruit these relatively few cases. This, he concluded, suggested "the possibility of change in some gay men and lesbians" but also that sexual reorientation "may be a rare or uncommon outcome of reparative therapy."

After eliminating 74 whose behavior and identity had changed but not their attraction, Spitzer conducted lengthy interviews with the remaining 200. Of these, slightly less than half of both the men and women recalled being "exclusively homosexual" before the change effort, and only 17 percent of the men were and 54 percent of the women were "exclusively heterosexual" after. Moreover, nearly half the males who masturbated still had occasional same-sex fantasies after their "change." Reflecting on the difficulty of finding self-proclaimed ex-gays, and on the seeming difficulty of complete transformation, Spitzer concluded: "To my horror, some of the media reported the study as an attempt to show that homosexuality is a choice, and that substantial change is possible for any homosexual who decides to make the effort. . . . In fact, I suspect that the vast majority of gay people would be unable to alter by much a firmly established homosexual orientation."

Such interview research suffers the problems of human recall. Time and again, researchers have observed participants in weight-control, antismoking, academic-skills, and delinquency-prevention programs testifying to substantial benefits. "This program changed my life!" Yet time and again, when the participants' actual behavioral barometers (weight, smoking habits, grades, arrest records) are compared with those of comparable people in an untreated control group, no therapeutic effect is evident.

There is an understandable reason for the misleading self-reports: memories are malleable and fallible. As they recall their histories and report their present, people tend to justify what they want to believe. We author and revise our life stories in the context of our current beliefs and attitudes. Thus, noted the late evangelical writer Mike Yaconelli, "every moving illustration, every gripping story, every testimony, didn't happen (at least, it didn't happen like the storyteller said it happened)."[29] Having expended time, effort, money, and ego on a change effort, people are highly motivated to think, "I may not be perfect now, but I was worse before. This did me a lot of good."

Data published by sex researchers Masters and Johnson in 1979 are also still cited by some ex-gay ministries who claim they can help homosexual persons leave homosexuality. Masters and Johnson had worked with clients and their opposite-sex partners who reported dissatisfaction with their homosexuality and a desire to function heterosexually.[30] These clients were strongly motivated (many were in marriages and some were likely bisexual), and the Masters and Johnson two-week daily therapy program proved effective for 29 out of 67 clients, in that these individuals were helped in terms of *behavior*. However, their fantasies, dreams, and erotic arousal were not taken into account, which other sex researchers view as a serious flaw in the research and in the conclusions often drawn from it. Being able to function or "perform" heterosexually need not signify a conversion to heterosexuality.

Given the problems with retrospective testimonials—even snake oil received glowing testimonials—what's needed, Spitzer agrees, is some sort of "prospective" experiment comparable to drug-efficacy experiments. (Whether such an experiment would be feasible or desirable is another question.) To assess the efficacy of a diet drug, for example, one would never just solicit testimonials from a relatively small number of people who claim to have lost weight after taking the drug (trusting their recall and not counting those who hadn't lost weight). Thus, the necessary if impractical experiment would

> identify male volunteers wishing to undergo sexual reorientation and measure their genital sexual responses to same- and other-sex erotic stimuli (to verify sexual attraction solely to same-sex stimuli);
> randomly assign some to a proposed treatment (perhaps reparative therapy as part of a transformation ministry) and the others to a waiting list;
> after the treatment, reassess sexual orientation by the same physiological measure.

If many of the treated volunteers evidenced a reversed sexual attraction, and if this result could be sustained and then confirmed by another research team, the skeptics could be refuted.

If American Family Association president Donald Wildmon was right when he said that the national "Coming out of Homosexuality Day" dispelled "the lies of the homosexual rights crowd who say they are born that way and cannot change," then perhaps he would welcome such an experiment.[31] But he likely was given pause when Michael Johnston, the national chair of Coming out of Homosexuality Day and a featured "ex-gay" spokesperson in TV and print ads, closed his ministry and ceased organizing the day after acknowledging that he had recently engaged in sexual encounters with other men.[32]

"Can leopards change their spots?" asked the prophet Jeremiah (13:23). Well-meaning people of faith will continue to struggle with new forms of Jeremiah's question as they seek grace to accept with serenity what cannot be changed, courage to change what should be changed, and the wisdom to discern the one from the other.

Seven

What the Bible Does and Doesn't Say

The Word has to be free to remake and reform the Church over and over again.
—G. C. Berkouwer, "Understanding Scripture," *Christianity Today,* 1970

THE ONE IMPORTANT REASON many Christians insist that gays and lesbians change their orientation is the belief that the Bible unequivocally condemns homosexuality. Some people of faith see no need for further discussion. Isn't the matter settled for all time? "God says it's wrong. It's an abomination. Case closed."

But is it? Discussions of the Bible and homosexuality usually center around either a handful of selected Scripture verses or around a theology of creation, gender, and marriage. We believe it's important to examine both of these approaches. Only then can we answer the question, is the case closed? In this chapter, we'll look at the Scripture verses most often used by those who believe the Bible condemns homosexual relationships. Then, in chapter 9, we'll deal with questions about creation, gender, and marriage.

The word *homosexuality* is never used in Scripture. In fact, the word didn't even exist until late in the nineteenth century.[1] In the few places where same-sex sexual *acts* are mentioned in Scripture, the context suggests idolatry, violent rape, lust, exploitation, or promiscuity. Nothing is said about homosexual *orientation* as understood through modern science, nor is anything said about the loving relationship of two same-sex persons who have covenanted to be life partners. It's important to keep those distinctions in mind when examining the small number of biblical passages commonly used in discussions of homosexuality.

Scripture Texts from the Old Testament

Genesis 19 The destruction of Sodom and Gomorrah, recorded in Genesis 19, is often cited as evidence of God's judgment upon homosexuality. Our English words *sodomy, sodomite, and sodomize* originated in such an interpretation. Here is a summary of the story.

Abraham's nephew, Lot, had recently moved to the city of Sodom. In the New Testament, written many centuries later, we're told that Lot had been a godly man who was deeply distressed by the evil around him in his new home (2 Pet. 2:7–8). One day, God and two angels, appearing as three men, visited Abraham to announce that Abraham's wife Sarah would bear a son. A little later, there was another announcement: God was planning to destroy Sodom because of its wickedness. The nature of that wickedness is detailed in the book of Ezekiel, where God says, "Sodom's sins were pride, laziness, and gluttony, while the poor and needy suffered outside her door. She was proud and did loathsome things, so I wiped her out, as you have seen" (Ezek. 16:49–50, NLT).

Concerned for his nephew and family now living there, Abraham started bargaining with God. He boldly appealed to God's fairness and justice. If a certain number of righteous people were in the city, shouldn't it be spared for their sakes? God agreed. The negotiations then centered around how *many* righteous people were necessary for the city to get a reprieve. When ten was the agreed-upon final number, the two angels went to Sodom to look for ten righteous persons.

In Sodom, Lot invited the angel-men to his home, where he treated them warmly and prepared a feast. But after the meal, before they settled down for the night, there was a great commotion outside. A mob composed of every man in the city, young and old, had surrounded Lot's house, shouting, "Where are the men who came to you tonight? Bring them out to us, so that we may know them" (Gen. 19:5).

At this point, both interpretation and translation come into the picture. How we understand the rest of the story hinges on the meaning of the word *know* in the verse just quoted. Is it a euphemism for sexual relations, or might it mean something else? Bible scholars and translators have often disagreed.

Nonsexual interpretation of the Sodom story   Don Blosser, a Mennonite New Testament scholar, points out that "know" is a translation of a Hebrew word that occurs more than a thousand times in the Old Testament. But it serves as a euphemism for sexual intercourse no more than eleven times. Scholars debate whether this is one of those times.[2]

If the phrase "that we may know them" means that the men of Sodom wanted to check out Lot's guests for other than sexual reasons—perhaps suspicious that these strangers might be hostile spies threatening their homeland security—the passage may have nothing at all to do with same-sex eroticism. It may simply mean that the mob was suspicious because Lot, the newcomer, had invited strangers into his home without having cleared them properly with the city authorities. "This fellow came here as an alien, and he would play the judge!" they shouted when Lot implied that he knew that his guests were men worthy of his hospitality and protection (Gen. 19:9). The men of Sodom may have been declaring in no uncertain terms that they wanted to investigate the visitors as possible illegal aliens up to no good.

Sexual interpretation of the Sodom story   On the other hand, Lot's offer of his two virgin daughters to the mob may suggest a sexual element. But this offer says nothing about homosexuality as an orientation. It only shows a low regard for women. (A similar story is found in Judges 19, where a woman is thrown out to such a mob and is repeatedly gang-raped, to the point of death.) Furthermore, if every male in the city was acting out of an erotic desire for *men,*

Lot's offer of two women wouldn't likely be regarded as a substitute. The men in the mob appear to have been driven by something more than simply a craving for sexual thrills (although they may have been aroused by the thought of using sex as a weapon).

A desire to sexually humiliate the visitors and submit them to gang rape is a likely possibility. Such intentions may explain the mob's unruly efforts to break down Lot's door. Rape of any sort is an act of violence. Male rape, as a show of power and domination, has a long history. According to the National Center for Victims of Crime, "the rape of a defeated male enemy was considered the special right of the victorious soldier in some societies and was a signal of the totality of the defeat. There was a widespread belief that a male who was sexually penetrated, even if it was by forced sexual assault, thus 'lost his manhood' and could no longer be a warrior or ruler."[3]

Similar attitudes apparently lay behind the 2004 Abu Ghraib military prison scandal in Iraq, in which a number of U.S. soldiers photographed the various methods they used to sexually humiliate male Iraqi prisoners, including forcing the men to simulate sex acts with each other, wear women's underwear, and, in at least one case, submit to rape.[4] Another much-publicized incident of sexual assault was the 1999 police brutality case in which a Haitian immigrant was brutality raped with a broken stick by a New York City police officer.[5] And in still another incident, the 2003 football season at Mephram High School on Long Island was canceled after three young junior varsity football players were held down and forcibly penetrated by older members of the football team, using a broomstick, pine cones, and golf balls, while other players watched and considering it hazing rather than a violent criminal act. One boy required surgery afterward, and the emotional scarring of such victims is lasting.[6]

Stephen Donaldson, former president of Stop Prisoner Rape,[7] learned about such sexual humiliation in a painfully personal way after he was arrested during a 1973 Quaker "pray-in" at the White House to protest the bombings in Cambodia. Although he was later acquitted, he spent time in jail and was gang-raped repeatedly and contracted AIDS, which years later cost him his life. In a *New York Times* article about prison rape, he pointed out that "the victims are usually heterosexuals who are forced into a passive sexual role, though the relatively few known homosexuals are perhaps three times as likely to be raped. The assailants are almost always heterosexual by preference; thus the phrase 'homosexual rape' is extremely misleading."[8] Such same-sex prison rapes are about power, control, humiliation—a way of supposedly proving one's manhood by robbing another of his through forcing him into what is considered the inferior, female role. Rape, whether of a male or a female, is always an act of power and violence rather than a sexual expression. It is important to remember this in considering possible sexual implications in the story of Sodom's destruction.

Leviticus 18:22 and 20:13　Those who believe that the Bible leaves no doubt about the sinfulness of homosexuality often cite two passages from Leviticus (both addressed to men). Leviticus 18:22 says, "You shall not lie with a male as with a woman; it is an abomination." Commenting on this verse and a similar verse, Leviticus 20:13 (the latter with a death penalty attached), *The Jewish Study Bible* has this note: "Biblical and ancient Near Eastern culture was not familiar with homosexuality in the sense of a defined sexual orientation or lifestyle (according to the biblical evidence David and Jonathan had no sexual relationship). It acknowledges only the occasional act of male anal intercourse, usually as an act of force associated with humiliation, revenge, or subjection."[9] (The Old Testament did not address same-sex acts between females.)

It's important, then, not to use these verses in Leviticus 18 and 20 as "proof texts" to argue that God strongly condemns all same-sex expression or that the word *abomination* in these verses indicates that homosexual acts are uniquely detestable in God's sight. The word translated as "abomination" is used often in Scripture to condemn lying, unjust business practices, pride, and stirring up dissension.[10] It is regrettable that in some religious circles, the word *abomination* is cruelly and self-righteously hurled at homosexual persons while the message of Proverbs 16:5 ("All those who are arrogant are an abomination to the Lord") is ignored.

It's also important to recognize that the Bible is a collection of various types of literature written over more than a thousand years and addressing many different cultural situations. The Bible contains history, laws, poetry, prophecy, stories (many in parable form), letters to individuals and congregations, and more. Some people who have simply heard *The Bible says. . .* about a certain topic may assume that the Bible is like a list of traffic laws in a driver's manual. They may consider it a compilation of rules applicable for all times, places, and situations. But, for instance, the often quoted Leviticus verses were part of ancient Israel's holiness codes given for *specific* purposes. One purpose was to distinguish the people of Israel from the surrounding nations, which practiced idolatry. Israel must be different. (See the opening and closing verses of Leviticus 18.) If we are to understand, interpret, and apply biblical teachings, we must view them in historical and cultural context.

Some rules given to the people of Israel were moral laws (such as are found among the Ten Commandments—laws such as "Thou shalt not bear false witness" and "Thou shalt not steal"). Other laws were specifically related to the criminal and civil justice systems of ancient Israel—for example, specific rules and penalties about rape, murder, adultery, and liability. (Some of the penalties attached to certain behaviors would be considered cruel and unreasonable punishment in our culture and time. For example, if a woman tried to rescue her husband during a fight with another man and in the process grabbed the opponent's genitalia, the woman's hand was ordered to be cut off without pity [Deut. 25:11].) There were instructions about such matters as divorce and remarriage (Deut. 24:1–4), not charging interest on loans to other Israelites (Deut. 23:19), the treatment of slaves (Deut. 23:15), paying workers fairly and promptly (Lev. 19:13; Deut. 24:14–15), harvesting fields in such a way that some food was left for poor people to find (Lev. 19:9–10; 23:22), and so on.

Some laws were built around the concept of ceremonial purity so that the people of Israel would be clearly distinguished from the nations around them. Such rules were part of a complex system emphasizing lessons of symbolic wholeness, perfection, and being set apart. For example, there were detailed rules about ceremonially clean and unclean foods (Lev. 11), about shaving (Lev. 19:27), about tattooing (Lev. 19:28), about a woman's ceremonial uncleanness during menstruation and after childbirth, and about a man's ceremonial uncleanness if he had an emission of semen (Lev. 15). The holiness code included rules about separating objects not considered to belong together. There were prohibitions against mixing two types of seeds during planting, plowing with an ox and a donkey yoked together, wearing garments made of two different fabrics (Lev. 19:19), and wearing clothing made for persons of the other gender (Deut. 22:5).

Sexual intercourse during a woman's menstrual period was considered an abomination (Lev. 18:19, 20:18) no less than a male's lying with another male as with a woman (Lev. 18:22, 20:13). Both prohibitions were listed in the same passage as violations of purity, and therefore they were considered defiling. Such behaviors were associated with the nations that had served other gods and that had to be driven out because they had "defiled the land" with their detestable practices (Lev. 18:24–30). Yet various conservative Christians, Tim and Beverly LaHaye among them, who have insisted that same-sex sexual acts are an abomination, have nevertheless counseled modern couples to have sexual intercourse during the wife's menstruation.[11]

Most people of the Christian faith believe that the purity laws and other rules given to the people of ancient Israel served a purpose for a particular time but, in view of New Testament teachings, are no longer applicable. We need to be cautious about taking a few carefully selected verses out of context and absolutizing them for all time, unless we're likewise ready to insist that all the other regulations be followed as well. (Among persons of the Jewish faith, of course, many of these rules, such as the food regulations, continue to be observed. But even within the various branches of Judaism, there have been modifications in the meaning and application of certain ancient laws as they relate to modern times, one example being a disregarding of the instructions in Deuteronomy 21:18–21 to stone to death a rebellious son.)[12]

Deuteronomy 23:17; 1 Kings 14:24, 15:12, and 22:46; 2 Kings 23:7

Deut. 23:17 (in the King James Version)
There shall be no whore of the daughters of Israel, nor a sodomite of the sons of Israel.

Deut. 23:17 (in the New Revised Standard Version)
None of the daughters of Israel shall be a temple prostitute; none of the sons of Israel shall be a temple prostitute.

1 Kings 14:24 (in the King James Version)
And there were also sodomites in the land: they did according to all the abominations of the nations which the Lord cast out before the children of Israel.

1 Kings 14: 24 (in the New Revised Standard Version)
There were also male prostitutes in the land. They committed all the abominations of the nations that the Lord drove out before the people of Israel.

1 Kings 14:24 (in the New Living Translation Version)
There were even shrine prostitutes throughout the land. The people imitated the detestable practices of the pagan nations the Lord had driven from the land ahead of the Israelites.

Some Christians have expressed dismay that newer English translations of these passages from Deuteronomy and 1 Kings don't use the word *sodomite* as the King James Version did. Some have posted Web sites accusing modern translators of distorting Scripture and furthering the "homosexual cause" by substituting words like *cult prostitute, temple prostitute, shrine prostitutes, male prostitutes,* or simply *prostitutes* in these verses. But the fact is that the words *sodomite* and *sodomites* never appeared in these verses in the original language. We don't honor the Word of God by insisting on an erroneous translation because it's familiar or fits preconceived notions or prejudices.

Jewish and Christian scholars agree that the original Hebrew words in Deuteronomy 23:17 may have referred to prostitution, but if so, it was most likely heterosexual and possibly of a ritualistic type. Whether or not such rituals ever involved same-sex activity has been debated by scholars, but there is no proof of it. In fact, according to the notes in *The Jewish Study Bible,* the various passages sometimes cited from 1 and 2 Kings may not have been referring to *sexual* practices at all. These passages were mainly concerned with idol worship, as their context shows, and may have been referring to "foreign specialists, perhaps poets and musicians," who assisted in idolatrous rites.[13] In sum, biblical scholarship has made clear that these passages, although they contain words that were at one time mistranslated as "sodomite," either refer to some form of prostitution or, just as likely, to ritual activities (not necessarily sexual) performed by persons set apart to honor gods other than the God of Israel.[14] In any case, they are not passages about homosexual persons or homosexual orientation.

Scripture Texts from the New Testament

In the New Testament, four passages are usually cited in discussions of same-sex acts. None are from the Gospels, because, according to these recorded accounts of Jesus's life and ministry, he never discussed the topic. Even when Jesus talked about Sodom, he spoke only about its sins of inhospitality to strangers (Matt. 10:5–15; Luke 10:10–12).

The passages that are sometimes used in discussions of homosexuality are all from the Epistles, the letters written to local gathered groups of Christians or to particular Christian individuals and later deemed by the church to be worthy of inclusion in Scripture. After extensive study of the Greek language in which these

New Testament books were originally written, many biblical scholars are convinced that these passages have nothing to do with homosexual *orientation* and committed homosexual relationships as we know them today.

1 Corinthians 6:9–10 and 1 Timothy 1:9–10 Two of the Scripture passages (1 Cor. 6:9–10; 1 Tim. 1:9–10) are general lists of categories of persons who were considered unrighteous or lawless. There are other lists of vices in the New Testament (e.g., Gal. 5:19–21; Eph. 5:3–12; Col. 3:5–10), but the passages in 1 Corinthians and 1 Timothy are the only ones that apparently refer to some form of same-sex sexual behavior. And both passages have created a problem for Bible translators. There is no exact modern-day cultural equivalent for what was being discussed. Yet these passages have often been misapplied to all persons whose sexual orientation is directed toward the same sex. Here is 1 Corinthians 6:9–10 in the old familiar King James Version:

> Know ye not that the unrighteous shall not inherit the kingdom of God? Be not deceived: neither fornicators, nor idolaters, nor adulterers, nor *effeminate,* nor *abusers of themselves with mankind,* nor thieves, nor covetous, nor drunkards, nor revilers, nor extortioners, shall inherit the kingdom of God. (emphasis added)

Much of the difficulty lies in understanding two Greek words in the original texts. Both are found in 1 Corinthians 6:9. One of the words, *malakoi,* is the word the King James translators rendered as "effeminate." (In the Greek, it simply meant "soft" and was sometimes used to describe lazy, self-indulgent, decadent living.) The King James scholars translated the second of the two Greek words, *arsenokoitai,* with the phrase "abusers of themselves with mankind." Some biblical scholars tell us this second word was an unusual combination of the words for "male" and "bed" and that its exact meaning is not clear. Others have suggested that it might be a Greek word coined in reference to the Hebrew words used in the passages from Leviticus 18:22 and 20:13 discussed earlier in this chapter.[15]

After studying the cultural background and other literature of the period, New Testament scholar Robin Scroggs concludes that Paul was using those two words, *malakoi* and *arsenokoitai,* to describe a particular type of pederasty common in the Greco-Roman world.[16] An adult male would use a teenage boy for sexual gratification, an arrangement that often involved monetary payment or the exchange of material gifts. The youth then served as a type of male "mistress," "call-boy," or prostitute. Sometimes such sexual encounters occurred between teachers and their young male students.

1 Timothy 1:9–10   The Greek word that the King James translators rendered as "abusers of themselves with mankind" in the passage from 1 Corinthians also appears in the list of lawless and ungodly people in 1 Timothy 1:9–10:

> Knowing this, that the law is not made for a righteous man, but for the lawless and disobedient, for the ungodly and for sinners, for unholy and profane, for murderers of fathers and mothers, for manslayers, for whoremongers, for *them that defile themselves with mankind,* for men stealers, for liars, for perjured persons, and if there be any other thing that is contrary to sound doctrine. (emphasis added)

There, *arsenokoitai* was translated as "them that defile themselves with mankind" and appeared between two other words, translated as "whoremongers" and as "men stealers." What seems clear from both the passage in 1 Corinthians and that in 1 Timothy is that some of the males in these societies were engaging in *particular types of sexual activities* that were regarded as evil by both Jews and Christians. Professor Scroggs suggests that the writer of 1 Timothy was condemning the actual kidnapping of young boys by men who enslaved them for sexual purposes.

Scholars who want to translate the Bible for today's culture have been faced with a problem: how to present these complex ideas to a modern audience while using an economy of words. Some translators simply decided to combine the two Greek words and render them as one, the English word *homosexual.* They thereby created a host of new problems. Such a translation gave readers the impression that the Bible condemns all homosexual persons, even though homosexual orientation was not being discussed and was not even understood in the modern sense. There were other problems with such translations. The word *homosexual* would imply that women were being discussed, too, even though women were not included in what is described in these original texts. The practices described concerned only males. Furthermore, some persons who consider themselves homosexual lead celibate lives. What would such a translation, with its sweeping generalization, say to them?

Because we take the Bible seriously, we think it is important to show the problems that occur when translations obscure the meaning of a text rather than clarifying it—especially when a translation can be used in ways that cause harm. Sadly, we know of numerous homosexual persons who have contemplated or carried out suicide after having such passages repeatedly hurled at them like weapons.

1 Corinthians 6:9–10 as a case study   This passage can serve as an illustration of the translation problem—especially since it is the one often cited to argue that "homosexuals won't go to heaven." We've prepared a chart (Table 1) showing how the relevant words in this passage have been translated in several modern versions of the Bible.

The 1946 edition of the Revised Standard Version (RSV) translates these verses this way:

> Do you not know that the unrighteous will not inherit the kingdom of God? Do not be deceived; neither the immoral, nor idolaters, nor adulterers, *nor homosexuals,* nor thieves, nor the greedy, nor drunkards, nor revilers, nor robbers will inherit the kingdom of God. (emphasis added)

A footnote after the word *homosexuals* explains: "Two Greek words are rendered by this expression."

Later editions of the RSV and other modern versions show how translators have wrestled with the problem and have come up with different solutions. Here are thirteen examples:

Table 1. Variations in Translation Among Bible Versions

Bible Version	Translation of the Two Greek Words
New English Bible, 1961	"guilty of homosexual perversion" (combining the two Greek words)
Revised Standard Version, 1963	"sexual perverts" (combining the two Greek words)
Jerusalem Bible (Roman Catholic), 1966	"catamites" and "sodomites"
New International Version, 1973, 1974	"male prostitutes" and "homosexual offenders"
Today's English Version (Good News Bible), 1976	"homosexual perverts" (combining the two Greek words)
New Jerusalem Bible, 1985	"the self-indulgent" and "sodomites"
New Revised Standard Version, 1989	"male prostitutes" and "sodomites"
Revised English Bible, 1989	"sexual pervert" (combining the two Greek words)
Contemporary English Version 1995	"pervert" and "behaves like a homosexual"
Oxford New Testament Inclusive Version, 1995	"male prostitutes " (combining the two Greek words)
New Living Translation, 1996	"male prostitutes" and "homosexuals"
Today's New International Version, 2001	"male prostitutes" and "practicing homosexuals"
New English Translation, 2003[17]	"passive homosexual partners" and "practicing homosexuals"

Readers not trained in the original languages and biblical scholarship depend on translations for their understanding of what Scripture passages mean. But because of the difficulties involved in translating the particular passages discussed here, it's important to exercise caution before using them to pass judgment on gay and lesbian persons today.

The Book of Jude

> And the angels which kept not their first estate, but left their own habitation, he hath reserved in everlasting chains under darkness unto the judgment of the great day. Even as Sodom and Gomorrha and the cities about them in like manner, giving themselves over to fornication, and going after strange flesh, are set forth for an example, suffering the vengeance of eternal fire. (Jude 6–7, KJV)

Jude was concerned about sexual immorality during the love feasts of the early church. He wrote that intruders were "pervert[ing] the grace of our God into licentiousness" (v. 4). There is no reason to think that the sexual immorality described was anything but heterosexual. But verse 7 is sometimes quoted as evidence of God's judgment upon homosexual persons because it refers to the wrath of God poured out on Sodom and Gomorrah. A phrase in that verse has been translated as "pursued unnatural lust" (NRSV) or "perversion" (TNIV). The original Greek words are best translated as "went after other flesh." The King James Version had simply rendered it "going after strange flesh." In view of the context, where Jude reminded readers of a time when angels were punished for lusting after humans (Gen. 6), the meaning of "going after strange [or "other"] flesh" in Sodom possibly referred to humans lusting after the angel visitors. It is not a verse that can be reasonably applied to the question of homosexuality in our time.

Romans 1:26–27 After describing the idolatry of the Gentile world that had rejected Israel's God and turned to other gods, Paul wrote (as translated in two Bible versions):

> For this cause God gave them up unto vile affections: for even their women did change the natural use into that which is against nature: and likewise the men, leaving the natural use of the woman, burned in their lust one toward another; men with men working that which is unseemly, and receiving in themselves that recompense of their error which was meet. (Rom. 1:26–27, KJV)

> For this reason God gave them up to degrading passions. Their women exchanged natural intercourse for unnatural, and in the same way also the men, giving up natural intercourse with women, were consumed with passion for one another. Men committed shameless acts with men and received in their own persons the due penalty for their error. (Rom. 1:26–27, NRSV)

This passage, perhaps more than any other, is frequently quoted as proof of God's displeasure with homosexual acts, whether between women or between men. It is the only place in the entire Bible where women are mentioned in this connection. Even then, scholars have pointed out, it is not clear whether sexual expression *between two women* was the intended meaning. Did the words refer to lesbianism, or did they refer to women assuming a dominant position in heterosexual intercourse—which might have been considered unnatural behavior in a patriarchal society? Or might the women have been engaging in nonprocreative sexual acts and techniques that in themselves may have then been considered unnatural (possibly oral or anal sex with their male partners)? The words could be interpreted by Christians in these various ways, and have been over history.[18]

But, assuming that the passage *is* talking about same-sex sexual acts between women as well as men in a context of unbridled lust, idolatry, and promiscuity, does it say anything about homosexual orientation as it is now understood? Does verse 28, reading "and since they did not see fit to acknowledge God, God gave them up to a debased mind and to things that should not be done," speak at all to two gay men or two lesbians who *do* acknowledge God? What does the passage have to do with two same-sex persons who have never turned to other gods and who love and serve their Creator wholeheartedly, but who yet desire a faithful, committed relationship of the kind we are discussing in this book? And if these verses are silent about such a situation, how are we to understand and apply the passage in today's world? If same-sex sexual acts are considered unnatural ("against nature," as the King James Version puts it), what can be said to women and men of homosexual orientation who say that *heterosexuality* is unnatural for them? (Or for that matter, to heterosexual couples who express their love at times using the same sexual techniques as do homosexual couples.)

Many Bible scholars have concluded that this passage is not concerned with individual ethics but with a description of an entire culture that had rejected the true God.[19] That conclusion may not answer the questions posed here, but it might help us understand the particular argument that Paul was presenting in Romans. The major point of the argument was that the entire world had sinned and come short of God's glory and was in need of the salvation God freely offered by grace through faith (Rom. 3:23–24). This was the good news of the gospel of Jesus Christ to both Jew and Gentile (Rom. 1:16). New Testament scholar Reta Halteman Finger points out that the body of the book of Romans presented this argument in the form of a speech to be read aloud.[20]

The verses we've been looking at make up only a small subpoint of this section of Paul's argument. The *main* point was that God had simply let the people of the Gentile world go on with their sinful ways (given them over to their desires) because they had rejected God's revelation through the created world. They had turned to gods of their own making instead. Those included the god of lust, as shown in the phrase "consumed with passion." Christian ethicist Allen Verhey writes:

Homosexual behaviors were evidently understood by Paul . . . as prompted by an insatiable lust, the sort of lust which drives a man first to visit female prostitutes and then, in search of something more exotic, to seduce other men. There is clearly no concept of sexual orientation at work here. It may be an anachronism to import a notion of sexual orientation into the first century and into our reading of Paul, but it requires no anachronism to suggest that Paul refers here to homosexual behaviors freely chosen by people whose appetite for sexual pleasure was once but is no longer sated by heterosexual relationships.[21]

Many behaviors of that idolatrous world (including but not limited to sexual practices) were abhorrent to the law-observant Jews. Such lists of repulsive actions and attitudes were familiar to them and had been written about elsewhere.[22] Here were vices they could readily recite in judging and condemning others. Hearing or reading such lists would give them a sense of pride that they were different from those societies around them that had rejected the one true God.

But then, according to Reta Finger, Paul in a sense turned the tables and addressed the privileged, law-abiding Jew who boasted of keeping all of God's requirements. Paul, a Jew himself, asserted that such a person had no room to judge others. *Every* person is guilty before God, and "all, both Jews and Greeks, are under the power of sin" (Rom. 3:9). In view of the case Paul was developing in this discourse, it's important to avoid pulling out verses 26 and 27 from the first chapter of Romans and assigning them an importance and meaning far beyond what Paul apparently intended. Context is crucial. Otherwise, we are not being faithful to Scripture.

How the Early Church Dealt with Divisions Among Believers

Reta Halteman Finger suggests that as people of faith struggle over the question of homosexuality today, they might find it more helpful to concentrate on the fourteenth and fifteenth chapters of Romans rather than the first chapter. These chapters provide a case study of other, differing viewpoints that were hindering community within the early Christian church.

Bitter divisions were taking place between Gentile Christians and those Christians from Jewish backgrounds who strongly believed that the Torah's requirements of dietary rules and observances of special days must continue as part of the Christian faith. Finger points out how important these practices were to Jewish daily life both socially and in business dealings. They were "boundary markers separating Jews from Gentiles. Those who observed these rules were part of the people of God; those who did not were outside." Finger writes:

> Paul had dedicated himself to bringing the gospel to Gentiles and to breaking down the walls between Jew and Gentile— and this involved abandoning the boundary-markers of circumcision, food laws, and observance of sabbaths and special religious days. This would have been little problem for Gentiles who had never practiced these laws, but for those whose very identity was bound up with them, the crisis must have been monumental.[23]

Knowing how deep the emotions on these issues were running, Paul provided advice that was sensitive to both sides. Neither side was to pass judgment on the other. Persons who had embraced the Christian faith, regardless of whether their background was Jewish or Gentile, must be convinced in their own minds and act according to their own consciences on these particular issues. To do otherwise would be sin. And at the same time, they were to respect their sisters and brothers in Christ who were convinced differently and acting according to *their* consciences.

On a similar note, Don Blosser calls attention to the early church's divisions over accepting uncircumcised Gentiles into the family of faith. In that instance, the church leaders had to make decisions about whether the Gentile converts must first become

Jews (with circumcision as the outward sign) before they could become Christians. A special church conference was held to decide the issue, and the leaders came to an agreement that "they would no longer demand the ancient religious tradition of circumcision as a requirement for membership in the people of God." The issue was resolved, as Blosser points out, because the early church believed that God's Spirit was leading them "in a new direction and was challenging a practice that had always been a central declaration of Jewish faith." Asking rhetorically what it was that gave these Christians the authority to make such a change, he provides this answer:

> The Holy Spirit confronted them in the form of persons who had experienced the grace of God. This challenged them to re-examine how they had been reading some specific texts in the Scriptures. As they read the texts in light of this new experience of God's grace, they came to a new understanding.[24]

We might also want to think about the story of Peter's vision in Acts 10, in which God pronounced formerly forbidden foods as now acceptable, using this vision to awaken Peter to God's welcoming of Gentiles. Captain Cornelius of the Roman Army was in a sense a prototype of those who had been considered "other"— people whom Jews had been instructed to shun (Acts 10:27)—but who nevertheless had *not* exchanged the worship of the true God for false gods. Cornelius had been worshipping God alone and deserved to be accepted as a member of God's family, even though Peter and others had understood Scripture to exclude Gentiles. In his vision, Peter had argued with God about dietary rules, telling God he couldn't eat something that God had pronounced in Scripture to be unclean—even though God was now telling him to eat it. Now he had to acknowledge a new understanding, not only about food, but about Gentile people as well. It wasn't easy for Peter to give up long-held assumptions, but getting to know Cornelius made all the difference, so that Peter was able to proclaim, "I truly understand that God shows no partiality, but in every nation anyone who fears him and does what is right is acceptable to him" (Acts 10:34–45).

Might not this same thing be happening today as heterosexual people of faith are getting to know devout gay and lesbian people of faith and being forced to reconsider long-held assumptions and interpretations of Scripture? Not only is this development opening up questions of welcoming gay and lesbian believers into our churches as both members and leaders, but it is also opening up questions about same-sex marriage, including the theological questions it raises about our Creator's intent in creating humankind as male and female and providing the institution of marriage.

We'll be discussing these matters in the next two chapters, but for now, it might be useful to review these major points:

- The Bible has very little to say about same-sex sexual expression.
- The few verses that speak of same-sex acts must be seen *in their context* and in relation to the condemnation of idolatry, lust, promiscuity, and exploitation.
- Translators have muddied the waters in many cases, because the specific behaviors that were addressed in their cultural context don't easily lend themselves to a succinct and descriptive rendering in modern English.
- Scripture does not speak to naturally disposed same-sex orientation, nor does it speak to loving, committed homosexual relationships.
- Jesus is not recorded as having said anything at all about homosexuality, but he said a great deal about loving our neighbor, being humble, avoiding judgmentalism, and caring about people who were hurting and regarded as outcasts. "The least of these" in any category of humankind were very important to Jesus (Matt. 25:31–46). Shouldn't we, then, as followers of Jesus, be asking what Jesus would do about the questions raised by our homosexual brothers and sisters as they seek out their role in the family of God? How would

Jesus regard a loving, committed same-sex couple? What did he, as the Word made flesh, have on his radar screen, and what should we therefore have on ours? These are the questions we need to keep in mind as we approach the question of same-sex marriage.

Eight

What God Has Joined Together?

Homosexuality is a burden that homosexual people are called to bear, and bear as
morally as possible, even though they never chose to bear it. . . . It is a burden most
obediently and creatively borne in a committed love-partnership with another.
Lewis Smedes, *Sex for Christians* and personal correspondence

VISITING SAN FRANCISCO City Hall in early 2004, the essayist
Richard Rodriguez, speaking on PBS's *NewsHour,* was deeply moved:

> Homosexual couples lined up around the block, thousands of
> them, waiting for a word on a certificate: "Marriage." . . .
> [These same-sex partners] wanted to be recognized by the
> community as promising fidelity to one another. The mood of
> those days was nothing like I had ever seen in gay America.
> What began as a rebellious political gesture had turned
> earnest. By contrast, in the gay day parades of summer, every
> sort of eccentricity and irony and nonconformity is accepted in
> the defiant celebration of one's right to proceed as "I."

What was happening at city hall (later to be overturned by the
California Supreme Court) was different; the emphasis was clearly
on *we*. There was no sign "of the gaudy or of camp," Rodriguez said.
The mood was one of "joyful determination to be acknowledged as
couples by the civic family." And the people seemed so ordinary. "I
also saw your uncle there at city hall," he continued, "your niece,
your cousin, your accountant, your clergyman, members of our

American family—he and he; she and she. People who have inter-
nalized a huge burden of loneliness in their lives suddenly stepped
forward in the light of day to announce themselves publicly. Each
said 'I do,' searching in America for 'we.'"[1]

This sense of *we,* this longing for belonging, has been a theme
running through this book. And yet there are those, many of
whom claim to be carrying out God's will, who put great effort
into preventing same-sex couples' commitment from being sealed
in marriage. Legal challenges to gay marriage are often fueled by
deeply felt religious fervor. The pain these efforts inflict on many
gay and lesbian people is tremendous.

Del Martin and Phyllis Lyon, the first same-sex couple to be
married during the month in which such marriages were permitted
in San Francisco, were reported to have been devastated when the
court ruling nullified their marriage. "Del is 83 years old, and I am
79," Phyllis Lyon said. "After being together for more than 50 years,
it is a terrible blow to have the rights and protections of marriage
taken away from us. At our age, we do not have the luxury of time."[2]

Since religious groups are so often at the forefront of opposition to same-sex marriage, we need to explore what various people
of faith believe is God's intent regarding gender and marriage. In
the preceding chapter, we saw that some Christians who are convinced that God condemns all same-sex relationships base their
belief on interpretations of certain biblical passages. Other Christians draw similar conclusions from their understanding of God's
intention in creating humans as male and female and uniting them
in heterosexual marriage. Still others accept alternatives to both
approaches and have arrived at different conclusions.

God, Gender, and Marriage

The question of how people of faith see marriage in relation to
God is related to two contrasting views or paradigms. In one paradigm, marriage is defined by the unique type of couple relationship it signifies. In the other paradigm, marriage is defined not
only by the unique type of couple relationship it signifies *but also by*

the gender of the adults who make up the relationship. If we were to put the two views in a chart, it would look something like Table 2:

Table 2. Two Paradigms Showing the Essential Ingredients for Marriage

	Paradigm A	Paradigm B
Characteristics	Economic interdependence	Economic interdependence
	Sexual/romantic interdependence	Sexual/romantic interdependence
	Commitment (pledge of exclusiveness and permanence)	Commitment (pledge of exclusiveness and permanence)
	Public declaration	Public declaration
	Compliance with requirements for legal recognition (licensing, etc.)	Compliance with requirements for legal recognition (licensing, etc.)
	Officially granted privileges, rights, and responsibilities of marriage	Officially granted privileges, rights, and responsibilities of marriage
Possibilities for children to become part of the family	Biological reproduction, including use of assistive reproductive technology	Biological reproduction, including the use of assistive reproductive technology
	Adoption	Adoption
	Stepchildren from either or both of the spouses' former marriages	Stepchildren from either or both of the spouses' former marriages
The parties who make up the marriage	Man + Woman	Person + Person (Usually Man + Woman. Also Woman + Woman, or Man + Man)

The Gender Issue

Everything is essentially the same in both paradigms in table 2 except for the last row. Paradigm A highlights gender—something that many people, believing that God cannot be present in the uniting of two men or two women, see as a religious concern. To them, the gender makeup is indeed the bottom line—not only in the paradigm chart, but in life. God, they believe, made the two sexes to *complement* each other. Therefore, *only* the uniting of a man and a woman can be considered a marriage. Their bodies are designed for such uniting, and children may result from the union.

What is more, in the thinking of many people, the sexual differences go far beyond the physical, encompassing an essential maleness and femaleness of mind and spirit that requires the two partners to be opposites. Procreation demands it, and a gendered creation and social order seem built upon presumed laws of nature.

Pittsburgh Theological Seminary professor Robert Gagnon, for example, believes—based on two passages in Genesis that Jesus quoted when asked about divorce—that "Jesus adopted a 'back-to-creation' model of sexuality." He bases his beliefs on Jesus's words as recorded in Mark 10:6–9:

> But from the beginning of creation, "God made them male and female." "For this reason a man shall leave his father and mother and be joined to his wife, and the two shall become one flesh. So they are no longer two, but one flesh." Therefore what God has joined together, let no one separate.

"In contending for the indissolubility of marriage," says Gagnon, "Jesus clearly presupposed the one explicit prerequisite in Gen. 1:27 and 2:24; namely, that there be a male and female, man and woman, to effect the 'one flesh' reunion." This reunion, Gagnon explains, is of the two halves of the first human creature, "an originally binary, or sexually undifferentiated, *adam* ('earthling')," split apart into two sexes in the Genesis 2 account of the creation of humankind. Gagnon believes that this incompleteness of one sex without the other is evidenced by the fact that only a very tiny percentage of people seek same-sex mates. The vast majority of people seek mates of the other sex. Men desire women; women desire men. "All this," he says, "indicates a basic societal admission that there is an essential and holistic maleness and femaleness that transcend mere social constructs."

But couldn't an argument be made just as easily about the small percentage of people who *do* seek same-sex mates? Might not their very existence among both humans and animals demonstrate that heterosexuality is not inevitable—that there is room for variation in sexual orientation as in handedness? (As we noted in chapter 5, there may be biological wisdom behind varying sexual orientation.) For Gagnon, however, the matter goes beyond observing the dominant social pattern: "Marriage is not just about more intimacy and sharing one's life with another in a lifelong partnership," he insists. "It is about sexual merger—or, in Scripture's understanding, *re*-merger—of essential maleness and femaleness."[3]

However, Jesus's point in Mark 10:6–9 was not about sexual differentiation. In response to religious leaders hoping to trap him with a trick question, Jesus was talking about marital permanence as God's ideal. Reminding Jesus that Moses had permitted husbands to divorce their wives with ease, the leaders noted that "Moses allows a man to write out divorce papers and send his wife away." To this, Jesus replied, "Moses gave you this law because you are so heartless" (Mark 10:4–5, CEV). Jesus was talking about husbands and wives, males and females, who were already in a marriage relationship, *because that was what the religious leaders were asking about.* This was not a philosophical or theological discussion about sexual differences and the need for a merger between two incomplete halves. Jesus and Paul both spoke positively about singleness without any implication that not being married meant that a person was somehow not whole.

Richard Mouw, the president of Fuller Theological Seminary, has likewise argued that marriage "isn't created by human contracts, but it is something that was created by God as a lifelong faithful partnership between a man and a woman." Marriage, he says, serves not only "to propagate the human race and to promote healthy families within that propagation, but also to model the mental faithfulness between God and his people, and Christ and his church."[4] Mouw alludes to Ephesians 5, where the imagery suggests two ways of understanding the church—as a bride and as a body. In that passage, the creation story from Genesis 2 is quoted again as we're reminded that "a man will leave his father and mother and be joined to his wife, and the two will become one flesh." The writer of the epistle continues: "This is a great mystery, and I am applying it to Christ and the church" (Eph. 5:31–32). In other words, this is metaphorical language.

"The essence of a metaphor is understanding and experiencing one kind of thing in terms of another," write George Lakoff and Mark Johnson in *Metaphors We Live By.*[5] But what *is* the "one kind of thing" in Ephesians 5 that we are to understand and experience in terms of something else? Is the emphasis on sexual differences? Is this, then, a proclamation of an essential maleness and femaleness? Or is the emphasis on *relationship*—specifically, a relationship of caring, love, intimacy, sacrifice, and oneness, a relationship that offered the potential of challenging the social order of that time (submissive wives and dominant husbands) and of moving it toward an equal partnership in which the two marriage partners mutually submit to each other in love? If the emphasis is on the latter, could it not be argued that two persons of the same sex, equally committed to each other, might also relate in this way?

Of course, some people—and whole societies—see gender distinctiveness as highly important. In various cultures and historical periods, male and female not only have been considered different in their essential nature, but also have been assigned different social roles, with women's role usually secondary—even in sexual intimacy. According to Bernadette Brooten, a professor of Christian studies at Brandeis University, "gender role transgression" was the major reason behind the negative attitudes sometimes expressed about female homosexuality within Greek and Roman culture during the time of the early Christians. She writes that "ancient shapers of culture" assumed that "a married woman was 'under a man' and saw homoerotic women as transgressing nature by experiencing pleasure while not under a man."[6] What were considered natural sexual roles required that "men 'do' or 'act,' while women 'suffer' or 'are passive.'"[7] For a woman to love another woman was considered to confound "this schema."[7]

Theologian Rosemary Ruether believes that using the notion of complementarity as a reason for insisting that "heterosexuality [is] the sole norm of healthy sexual relations" is harmful to both women and men. This concept of a psychic complementarity, based on different physical characteristics, "covertly demands the continued dependency and underdevelopment of women in order to validate the thesis that two kinds of personalities exist by nature in males and female and which are each partial expressions of some larger whole." The danger in this view, according to Ruether, is that it "can allow neither men nor women to be whole persons who can develop both their active and their affective sides."[8]

The notion of male dominance and female subordination is one of the areas in which many of today's Christians have reexamined and reinterpreted Scripture.[9] Such reinterpretation is based on what we now know about the ancient social order in which Paul and others wrote and how the Bible's own principles were even then providing the seeds for change—not only with regard to the equality of the sexes, but also with regard to the overturning of slavery and other social-justice issues.[10] This approach does not mean discarding or demeaning Scripture, but rather applying its principles to our day—just as Paul and the other biblical authors, guided by God's Spirit, applied spiritual principles to their cultures. As Margaret Nutting Ralph has emphasized, Scripture passages in which wives were told to be subordinate and slaves were told to obey their masters "do not mean the author is teaching the proper order of society"; rather, "given that order, the author is telling his readers how to behave so as to grow in holiness."[11]

Even so, some Christians today continue to insist on the argument of separate social roles. They believe that the Creator had distinct purposes beyond procreation in designing male and female, and that allowing same-sex marriages would disrupt that pattern. James Dobson, for example, refers to the writings of social critic George Gilder in arguing that "women hold *the* key to the stability and productivity of men." Dobson comments:

> When a wife believes in her husband and deeply respects him, he gains the confidence necessary to compete successfully and live responsibly. She gives him a reason to harness his masculine energy—to build a home, obtain and keep a job, help her raise their children, remain sober, live within the law, spend money wisely, etc. Without positive feminine influence, his tendency is to release the power of testosterone in a way that is destructive to himself and to society at large. . . . Successful marriages serve to "civilize" and domesticate masculinity, which is not only in the best interests of women, but is vital for the protection and welfare of the next generation.[12]

And what is it that women need from men? "Conversely, a woman typically has deep longings that can only be satisfied through a romantic, long-term relationship with a man. Her self-esteem, contentment, and fulfillment are typically derived from intimacy, heart-to-heart, in marriage," says Dobson.[13] That a woman might have other needs and might also find her self-esteem enhanced in ways other than marriage and family is ignored. Might she not also need support for her career and other interests just as her husband does? Many Christians believe that the key to a successful marriage is a *mutually* supportive relationship in all areas of life. They interpret Scripture differently, and some of them believe that two persons whose orientation is homosexual might also give each other such support.

Marriage as an Inclusive Institution

In Paradigm B of table 2, each couple, whether straight or gay, has entered into a relationship of fidelity and commitment that entails all the rights and responsibilities of marriage. Ideally, the relationship itself is a sacred covenant.

Scripture often describes the relationship between God and God's people as a covenant. Perhaps rather than thinking in terms of gender, we might instead consider the characteristics of that covenant. In Hosea 2, God describes the covenantal relationship in these terms: "I shall betroth you to myself for ever, I shall betroth you in uprightness and justice and faithful love and tenderness. Yes, I shall betroth you to myself in loyalty and in the knowledge of Yahweh" (Hos. 2:21–22, NJB). (The translators of this passage use words that are quite similar to those still used in Jewish liturgy.) Hosea 2, in the Contemporary English Version, lists these characteristics of the marriage covenant: justice, fairness, love, kindness, faithfulness, and a revelation of God's personhood ("Then you will truly know who I am").

Think about it. If these characteristics define an ideal marriage, might two homosexual persons likewise form such a union? Might two men or two women desire to commit themselves completely to each other in a pledge of permanence, integrity, respect for the other, fairness, self-giving love, tenderness, faithfulness, and self-disclosure, just as might a man and a woman? If we can think in those terms, might we remove the question mark from the title of this book, and accept these covenantal relationships as indeed a joining of two persons by God?

We introduced this chapter with Christian ethicist Lewis Smedes's statement that homosexuality is an unchosen burden that is most creatively and morally borne in either celibacy or covenantal relationships. In our (and his) Christian ethics, a moral approach to *heterosexuality* is likewise based on celibacy or covenantal relationships. The difference, of course, is that we straight folks never call our heterosexuality a burden, because it involves no stigmatizing of who we are and whom we love. Excluding gay people from marriage does stigmatize who they are and whom they love. In the next chapter, we suggest that welcoming same-sex couples into marriage will have positive benefits for them, for their families, and quite possibly even for the institution of marriage.

Nine

Gay Marriage

Let marriage be held in honor by all.
—Hebrews 13:4

THE ALARMS ARE SOUNDING:

"The future of our country hangs in the balance."
"Losing this battle means . . . losing American civilization."
"Western civilization itself seems to hang on this issue."

What is this enormous evil that threatens to destroy our civilization? Terrorist-delivered weapons of mass destruction? Global-warming-spawned drought, heat, and hurricanes? The unleashing of a mutant killer virus?

In voicing these alarms Senator Rick Santorum, writer Maggie Gallagher, and James Dobson, respectively, are referring to what their kindred spirit, Charles Colson, calls "the death of marriage and family as we have known it for thousands of years."[1] That death, they fear, would result from a same-sex marriage experiment that, in Colson's words, "will cripple our society and undermine families and children (the basic building block of our culture) in irreparable ways."[2]

Making the argument in more positive terms, President George W. Bush on the 2004 campaign trail expressed his conviction "that a traditional marriage—marriage between a man and woman—is an important part of stable families."[3] Indeed, heterosexual marriage *is* a vital part of healthy family life and the co-parenting of thriving children. As marriage advocates, we nevertheless have become persuaded that the case for same-sex marriage is more persuasive than the case against it. What is more, by unintentionally encouraging alternatives to marriage, opponents of gay marriage may be unwittingly undermining marriage itself.

Presenting a Case for Gay Marriage

One argument for gay marriage responds to conservative voices who cite evidence that gay men often engage in unhealthy behaviors. (Many gay people likewise point out the hazards of risky behaviors and multiple partners. These, of course, are also hazards for heterosexual people.) In the United States, gay males have reportedly suffered higher rates of AIDS than have their heterosexual peers and are exposed to other sexually transmitted diseases as well.[4] They also tend to have higher rates of attempted suicide.[5]

Marriage, the same conservative voices point out, is associated with healthy behaviors and emotions. It's true, as we've shown in the social science studies mentioned earlier, that married people do live with greater happiness, emotional stability, health, and longevity—and understandably so, given our need to belong.

Assume that the conservative voices are right—that much of today's homosexual behavior tends to be risky and less healthy than marriage-related behaviors. What conclusion might a social conservative then draw? That we should work to keep gays *un*-married—that we should support *less* commitment, covenant, monogamy, and fidelity? Or that we should support more? With some nine hundred thousand HIV-positive Americans (with male-to-male sexual contact involved in the highest proportion of HIV cases)[6] and with more than half a million Americans already killed by AIDS—a total that exceeds American combat deaths in all twentieth-century wars—might it be healthier to suggest that confining sexual expression to a committed monogamous relationship (marriage) is the ideal for gays as well as for straights?[7]

A healthy way to satisfy the human need to belong Yale University law professor William N. Eskridge suggests that the legalization of same-sex marriage could actually strengthen the institution of marriage. He notes that the current trend is toward states offering relationship options (marriage, civil union, domestic partnership, temporary cohabitation). The weakness with this approach, he points out, is that "generally, the menu allows partners with a lesser degree of mutual commitment to choose a regulatory regime that offers fewer benefits in return for easier exit from the relationship." So, should those who denounce "the homosexual lifestyle" become *advocates* of admitting gays to the social institution that offers a positive alternative to that lifestyle? In other words, should gay marriage continue to be viewed as the problem, or might it be viewed as a solution? Eskridge argues that "if traditionalists truly want to preserve marriage—not just homophobia—it's time for them to join forces with the gay-marriage activists in a common cause."[8]

And consider: If our sexual orientation, gay or straight, is something we did not choose and cannot change, that raises some important questions about how we should live. Should people with an unchosen heterosexual orientation marry but at the same time insist that people with an unchosen homosexual orientation live alone? Or should *all* people who have not been granted what the Apostle Paul called the "gift" of celibacy be supported in their desire to make a vow of commitment and fidelity?

Whatever our sexual orientation, we humans have a need to belong, and that need is profoundly met by a mutual covenant of lifelong partnership that's affirmed by law and culture—in a word, by marriage. "I think it's a safe bet that marriage and the prospect of marriage would improve gay people's health and happiness and general welfare much as it has improved straight people's," writes Jonathan Rauch in *Gay Marriage: Why It Is Good for Gays, Good for Straights, and Good for America.* "I believe it will ennoble and dignify gay love and sex as it has done straight love and sex; I believe it will close the book on the culture of libertinism and liberation and replace it with a social compact forged of responsibility. In all these respects—physical, spiritual, cultural—gay lives will be improved, at least somewhat but probably immensely."[9]

Rauch's speculation finds support not only in the growing recognition of our need to belong, but also in the few existing studies of gay and lesbian couples. "Overall," reports the Gottman Institute with regard to one of its studies:

> Relationship satisfaction and quality are about the same across all couple types (straight, gay, lesbian) that [John] Gottman has studied. This result supports prior research by Lawrence Kurdek and Pepper Schwartz: They find that gay and lesbian relationships are comparable to straight relationships in many ways.[10]

A study of 450 Vermont couples in civil unions, not yet published, confirms that their self-reported relationship happiness is "quite high."[11] Compared with heterosexual couples, gay and lesbian couples have experienced less support from family members, but they tend to enjoy more equitable relationships.[12]

Marriage, more than cohabitation, "changes the way you think about yourself and your beloved," note Linda Waite and Maggie Gallagher in *The Case for Marriage: Why Married People Are Happier, Healthier, and Better Off Financially*. "It changes the way you act and think about the future; and it changes how other people and other institutions treat you as well."[13] Marry someone, and you address your need to belong by attaching yourself to another individual. "I am my beloved's and my beloved is mine" (Song of Sol. 6:3). You also gain the benefits of that person's family support system and society's backing. Small wonder that so many gay and lesbian people long to have the opportunity for such connections and social legitimacy.

Achieving equal rights That combination of connectedness and social legitimacy known as marriage brings with it privileges and duties, rights and responsibilities. And its uneven availability raises questions about basic fairness and justice. What do you think: should life partners Jim and Tim or Meg and Peg, like their married next-door neighbors Bill and Jill, be able to

- file joint tax returns;
- leave an inheritance to one another tax free;
- make life-and-death decisions if the other is incapacitated;
- be included on one or the other's health-insurance plan;
- be granted family leave or bereavement leave in the case of the other's illness or death;
- have co-parental rights so that both partners are considered parents of their children in all situations;
- have hospital visitation rights;
- receive spousal discounts from auto clubs and other organizations offering family rates;
- have a legal system for equitably dissolving their relationship should it end?

If so, should they simultaneously be required to honor the obligations of marriage—to

- support one another and any children they may have;
- share financial responsibilities;
- not be able to simply walk away from the relationship?

Consider two real people who are longtime friends and neighbors of one of us. For fifteen years, Dave and Doug have been loyal partners, together tending their beautiful garden and also the garden of their church, a half block away (where Dave just completed a term as deacon and where Doug is just starting one). Both are gentle, beloved souls who participate actively in their neighborhood association and are welcomed into homes as what they are—a couple. Should Dave and Doug have the freedom to marry and to enjoy the same rights enjoyed by a pair of nineteen-year-olds who elope on impulse and get married by a Las Vegas Elvis impersonator? Should all of the rights and obligations on these lists be considered theirs just as much as if they were a married heterosexual couple—not to mention the same social acceptance?

Note that this is not an issue of "special rights" but one of equal rights conveyed by marriage. Unlike cohabitation, domestic partnerships, and even civil unions (each of which are separate from and unequal to marriage), same-sex marriage entails the same rights for *all* married couples, rights including all "1,138 federal statutory provisions" for which the General Accounting Office in 2004 reported that "marital status is a factor in determining or receiving benefits, rights, and privileges."[14]

But couldn't the same goals be reached through establishing a "separate but equal" arrangement—with "civil unions" offered to same-sex couples and marriage only to heterosexual couples? We think not. Here's why:

> *Civil union* implies toleration of something inferior. *Marriage* connotes full societal acceptance.
>
> Civil unions provide limited rights. Marriages, straight and gay, enjoy equality of rights.
>
> Civil unions are a form of "marriage lite" and a boost to the alternatives-to-marriage movement. Marriage advances *marriage* as an institution.

Responding to the Case Against Gay Marriage

If the case for gay marriage is (a) that marriage is healthier than its alternatives and (b) that all people should enjoy the same rights, what is the case against gay marriage? Gay-marriage opponents offer at least seven arguments. Each, we believe, is ill considered.

1. *"Same-sex 'marriage' is a contradiction in terms. Marriage is historically and by definition the union of a man and a woman."*

This argument begs the question. Moreover, the understanding of marriage has changed repeatedly since the time when, for example, King David had eight wives and ten concubines.[15] Its definition has changed not only from polygamy to monogamy, but from arrangement to romantic choice, from male headship to mutuality, and from stigmatizing both interracial marriage and remarriage after divorce to accepting them.

Marriage as we know it has undergone enormous changes even in the United States, both in terms of persons permitted to marry and in terms of what marriage signifies and requires. Historian Hendrik Hartog points out that our idea of marriage—that it should be built on the right of individuals to seek happiness in an ongoing relationship with whomever they choose—came about only after two centuries of struggle. "During the 1970s and 1980s," he writes, "the U.S. Supreme Court repeatedly affirmed that everyone (by which they then meant heterosexuals only) has a right to marry, as an individual right."[16] This was not always the case, and both society and its laws underwent many changes in bringing this situation about, including changing attitudes toward divorce and interracial marriage. Furthermore, as Hartog emphasizes, marriage had long existed on the basis of an unequal contract between the spouses—a "fundamental legal understanding of marriage as a relationship of power and subordination." Becoming a wife in the nineteenth century meant losing one's identity under the doctrine of "coverture." Who a woman was as an individual was considered subsumed under (or covered over by) her husband's identity. She could not control property, enter contracts, or even have the right to her own earnings. If the marriage ended, the husband had the right to custody of their children. But societal attitudes and laws have changed on these matters, and in other ways as well.

The question is, should our understanding of marriage change again? Or should marriage be defined not just by vows, fidelity, or children (all of which homosexuals can have) but also by its exclusion of homosexuals, as the proposed federal marriage amendment would require?

2. *"Marriage implies procreation, which gays simply can't do."*[17]

This often heard argument was voiced during the social hour after one of our public talks. Standing next to the questioner were two recently widowed and now happily remarried people in their seventies. If sterility disqualifies people from marriage and threatens the institution, then this heterosexual couple should have been scorned rather than celebrated. Marriage *is* about having and raising children, but it's doubtful that any reader of this book thinks it's only about that. Heterosexual couples who have chosen not to have children can be just as married as anyone else. So can postmenopausal women, infertile men, and couples who, because of injury or illness, cannot engage in sexual intercourse or conceive children in the customary manner. And some homosexual people do procreate. A gay or lesbian couple may have children of their own from former heterosexual marriages, or one or the other may become the biological parent of a child conceived through artificial insemination. In addition, many lesbians and gay men become parents through adoption.

3. *"Children need both a mother and a father."*

The conservative Family Research Council says that same-sex marriage "will open wide the door to homosexual adoption, which will simply lead to more children suffering the negative consequences of growing up without both a mother and a father."[18] (Foster parenting and adoption by gay and lesbian persons are already permissible in many states, and laws are in flux in others.) Gay marriage will also "encourage teens who are unsure of their sexuality to embrace a lifestyle that suffers high rates of suicide, depression, HIV, drug abuse, STDs, and other pathogens," argued Robert Benne and Gerald McDermott in *Christianity Today*[19] (apparently presuming that people choose or get recruited into their sexual orientation and that all gays and lesbians live an injurious lifestyle). "Some children of homosexual parents may turn out alright," acknowledges Charles Colson's *BreakPoint WorldView Magazine.* "But . . . mothers and fathers, filling their distinct roles, shape our identity."[20]

Co-parented children from intact families are indeed at lessened risk for various pathologies. Although it will be some time before we have studies of the children of *married* gay or lesbian couples, we can make the following statements:

- *Fact:* More than seven in ten same-sex-couple households identified in the 2000 U.S. Census had no children.[21] So for most gay and lesbian couples, the question is moot.

- *Fact:* Existing studies of children in father-absent homes are nearly all studies of unstable or single-parent homes.
- *Fact:* The children of two-parent lesbian homes appear to develop normally and to be advantaged over the children of single heterosexual parents.

   "Sexual identities (including gender identity, gender-role behavior, and sexual orientation) develop in much the same ways among children of lesbian mothers as they do among children of heterosexual parents," notes a 2004 American Psychological Association statement.[22] "Taken together, the data do not suggest elevated rates of homosexuality among the offspring of lesbian or gay parents," notes University of Virginia researcher Charlotte Patterson in a briefing paper for the association. Moreover, she says, "not a single study has found children of lesbian or gay parents to be disadvantaged in any significant respect relative to children of heterosexual parents."[23]

   Alice Bengel, now in her mid-thirties after being raised by a lesbian couple, recalls how unexceptional her childhood was. She and her moms "loved and quarreled and made up and made do just like any other family," she recalls. Although only one of them gave birth to her physically, "most people were hard-pressed to tell which one. It wasn't a secret, it just wasn't obvious." She found out later that most people weren't even curious but just accepted her as "Doris and Paula's little girl." Teachers didn't care which of the mothers signed her report card, and no matter what she did, said, or wanted, she found that her two mothers "presented a united front, and appealing to one against the other was futile." She summed up her childhood in these words:

   I had two people who cared about me, looked after me when I was sick, got on my case when I ditched my chores, cheered at my graduations and cried at my wedding. I defy anyone to look me in the eye and say there's something wrong with that.

So, to those who justify their opposition to gay adoptions and same-sex unions by claiming concern for the children, I say this: Thanks for your concern, but there's no need to worry about us. We're turning out great.[24]

- *Fact:* Many same-sex couples with adopted children are parenting mentally or physically challenged children, or previously neglected or abused children.

     Take, for example, the stories of some gay couples one of us knows personally. Gay partners Jeff and Gary traveled to China to adopt a little boy who as a one-year-old had been abandoned at a train station. Taken to an orphanage, he was discovered to be deaf. No one could communicate with him. Gary is deaf, too, and teaches at a school for deaf children in Texas. He and Jeff communicate with each other through American Sign Language. So when the two men visited the orphanage and the little boy watched them talk with their hands, his eyes brightened. He saw that there was a visual way to communicate, and he connected with them immediately, quickly learning how to sign. The two men were able to legally adopt him as co-parents, and he is the joy of his fathers' hearts.[25]

     In another example of adoption by a same-sex couple, "Daddy Michael" and "Daddy Chris," as their children call them, shower love on four siblings between the ages of three and eight. These children came from a background of neglect and abuse. Social services had become involved after one of the children at age two had somehow found his way to a supermarket, where he scavenged for food for his hungry tummy. Now in their new home, the three boys and a girl each have their own room, lots of love and attention, abundant learning opportunities, and a secure future.

- *Fact:* For children such as those described here, the pertinent question is not whether children of long-term traditional heterosexual marriages fare better than children of single parents, as so many conservatives like to assert. The real question is whether children at risk fare better when left in their previous circumstances or when adopted and co-parented, even if by a same-sex couple. If so, wouldn't destigmatizing the family and recognizing co-parents further enhance the chances for the well-being of these children? The American Academy of Pediatrics thinks so. In 2002, the organization adopted a statement in support of gays seeking to adopt a partner's child: "Children who are born to or adopted by one member of a same-sex couple deserve the security of two legally recognized parents."

4. *"Gays are promiscuous."*

"New study highlights homosexual promiscuity," headlined one Family Research Council mailing.[26] Should such findings—that gay "relationships" are less enduring than straight *marriages*—surprise anyone? Heterosexual nonmarital relationships, including cohabitation, are similarly less enduring than marriages. Therein lies part of the case for marriage, which curbs promiscuity.

Gay men do have more partners than straight men, though that's also not surprising given that gay men are nearly all unmarried, and straight men are mostly married. But isn't it true, many people wonder, that gay men are predisposed to lust for more partners? Psychologist David Schmitt and his colleagues asked more than sixteen thousand people (mostly university students) in fifty-two countries how many sexual partners they would like to have in the next month.[27] Among those not currently married or in a relationship, 29 percent of heterosexual men and 31 percent of homosexual men expressed a desire for more than one partner. The same was true of 6 percent of heterosexual and 4 percent of homosexual women. Ergo, the gender difference was huge; the sexual-orientation difference was trivial. This gender difference explains why, despite there being about half as many lesbians as gay men, lesbians were 57 percent of San Francisco's same-sex marriages, and why American lesbians are nearly twice as likely to be coupled (43 percent) as are gay men (24 percent).[28]

And who desires more frequent sex, thinks more about sex, masturbates more often, initiates more sex, and makes more sacrifices to gain sex? The answers to these and other such questions (among both heterosexual and homosexual populations) are men, men, men, men, and men.[29] If unmarried gay men have more uncommitted sex, reflects Steven Pinker, "they are simply men whose male desires bounce off other male desires rather than off female desires."[30]

5. *"If marriage is redefined to include two men in love, on what possible principled grounds can it be denied to three men in love?"*

So wondered columnist Charles Krauthammer in a *Time* essay.[31] Consider, too, the concerns of a prior era: "It could lead to sex with animals"; "It's unnatural"; "It's against the Bible"; "There should be a constitutional amendment banning it." Sound familiar? In an earlier era, the *it* referred not to gay marriage but to *interracial* marriage.

In dissenting from the Supreme Court's overturning of a Texas sodomy law, Justice Antonin Scalia wrote: "State laws against bigamy, same-sex marriage, adult incest, prostitution, masturbation, adultery, fornication, bestiality, are . . . called into question by today's decision."[32] Similar concerns were voiced in a Focus on the Family brochure: "The ultimate result of expanding the definition of marriage is that marriage would mean everything—and nothing."[33]

This domino theory assumes that if we give an inch, they'll take a mile. We heard this often during Vietnam War days: "If we don't stop Communism there, it may soon spread like cancer." Well, we didn't, but it hasn't. Variations on the domino theory appear in such clichés as admitting the camel's nose into the tent, providing an opening for the thin edge of the wedge, and starting the slide down a slippery slope. "Ban AK-47s and before you know it they'll be coming for your hunting rifles." "Curtail smoking in public places and soon they'll be telling us what we can eat." "Let libraries block children's Internet pornography access and soon a police state will be censoring the free flow of ideas."

But reasonable laws—all of which restrain our freedom—seldom cascade us down a slippery slope or trip a line of dominoes.

"Not every young woman who allows herself to be kissed before marriage ends up a hooker," chides sociologist Amitai Etzioni.[34] Censoring slander, false advertising, cigarette ads, and pornography on network TV has not threatened *The Catcher in the Rye*'s place on our library's bookshelves. Society always manages to draw a line.

As it happens, the dominoes of same-sex marriage on the one hand, and of polygamy and incest on the other, are ten feet apart. They're logically unrelated. Gay people are not asking for the right to marry everybody they love, notes Jonathan Rauch; they are asking only "for what all heterosexuals possess already: the legal right to marry *somebody* they love."[35] By making universal a simple rule of *one person, one spouse,* we can "defend monogamy without hypocrisy or inconsistency," he emphasizes. "Children, parents, childless adults and marriage itself are all better off when society sends a clear and unequivocal message that sex, love and marriage go together. Same-sex marriage affirms that message."[36]

Conservative columnist David Brooks concurs: "The conservative course is not to banish gay people from making such commitments. It is to expect that they make such commitments. We shouldn't just allow gay marriage. We should insist on gay marriage."[37]

6. *"Gay marriage will undermine traditional marriage."*

"If gays are allowed to marry, the institution of marriage will be degraded." In a 2004 *Los Angeles Times* poll, 55 percent of Americans responding agreed with this statement.[38]

To others, it's not obvious how allowing more people to marry will threaten marriage. They ask, shouldn't we aim to have more, not fewer, people married? Did letting women into Rotary Club weaken Rotary? Are straight couples less likely to get married and stay married if they know that gay couples can marry? Would giving an added 3 percent of the population the right to marry diminish the supply of available marriage licenses? Would it discourage the other 97 percent from marrying?

Robert Gagnon is among those who would prefer to see gay people believe that "for any given homosexual person hope exists for forming a heterosexual union."[39] But is he being realistic, or would such advice lead to many a failed marriage and broken heart? In her book *Silent Lives: How High a Price?* the human rights activist Sara L. Boesser wonders if the societal pressures for gay and lesbian people to pass as heterosexual may be one of the many factors contributing to a high divorce rate in the United States. She points out that "passing has caused many gay and lesbian people to enter [heterosexual] marriages that are doomed to failure because genuine physical attraction is not part of their marriage's possibility." She is convinced that "the divorce rate, and all its fall-out, would be lower if lesbian, gay, and bi[sexual] couples could, instead, marry the person they most love and are attracted to."[40] The state where, as we write, gays *can* marry (Massachusetts) is also the state with the nation's lowest divorce rate over the last five years.

And what really threatens marriage? Millions of heterosexuals and the celebrities they adore are "hooking up" on a whim. A third or more of babies in North America and northern Europe are born to unmarried parents. Pornography is a bigger business than professional football. "And the religious Right can't think of a better way to respond to these heterosexual travesties and 'save' the institution of marriage than by prohibiting a few gay couples from the rights and responsibilities of the institution?!" exclaims the gay evangelical therapist Ralph Blair.[41] In C. S. Lewis's *Screwtape Letters,* senior devil Screwtape advises his junior apprentice devil to corrupt by creating what today we might call WMDs (weapons of mass distraction) that divert attention from the real issues at hand: "The game is to have them all running about with fire extinguishers whenever there is a flood."

In Europe and North America, the flood that threatens the house of marriage is not gay marriage but heterosexual *non*marriage, including cohabitation, domestic partnerships, and other "marriage lite" alternatives to marriage, all of which promise to offer the benefits of partnership without the burdens of marriage. With gay marriage banned nearly everywhere, corporations increasingly are offering domestic-partnership benefits to gay couples—and then, to be fair, to heterosexual couples as well. By banning gay marriage, we make the increasingly visible unmarried gay couples "into walking billboards for the irrelevance of marriage," argues Rauch in his marriage-supporting case for gay marriage.[42] "The only way to arrest this slide," he adds, "is to level the playing field. Go back to Rule 1. In fact, reinforce it. 'If you want the benefits of marriage, *get married*—no exclusions, no exceptions, no excuses.' Adopt same-sex marriage, and the alternatives-to-marriage movement loses its main impetus overnight."

After the passage of Vermont's civil-union law, the University of Vermont withdrew its long-standing domestic-partner benefits for same-sex couples. To get the benefits, same-sex couples had to form civil unions, and heterosexual couples had to be married.[43] After same-sex marriage was legalized in Massachusetts, many of the state's companies and universities announced that they would discontinue domestic-partner benefits for unmarried gay and lesbian couples, thus reducing the pressure for comparable benefits for unmarried opposite-sex couples.[44] Create a marriage option for all, declare that domestic-partner benefit programs are no longer needed, couple the change with a national marriage-renewal movement supported by the White House bully pulpit, and cost- and values-conscious corporations would then gladly require marriage as a condition for partner benefits.

7. *"The Scandinavian experiment shows that gay 'marriage' weakens marriage."*

"According to an article by Stanley Kurtz, ever since Norway recognized same-sex marriages in 1993 (again by court decree), Norway has seen 'less frequent marriage, more frequent out-of-wedlock birth and skyrocketing dissolution,'" warned Charles Colson in a 2004 letter.[45] In varying words, this argument shows up repeatedly in anti-gay-marriage essays, debates, and Webcasts.

Actually, Norway and the other Scandinavian countries don't, as of this writing, offer gay marriage. They offer what we argue against—a "marriage lite" substitute: civil-union-like "registered partnerships." Moreover, reports the economist Lee Badgett, Scandinavia's rising cohabitation rates preceded the advent of partner laws.[46] Scandinavian cohabitation also functions differently than it has in the United States. After having a child, most Scandinavian couples marry—which explains why although in Norway half of children are born to unmarried parents, four out of five couples with children are married.

Gut Feelings Feed Moral Intuitions

Many people we talk with are mystified by the intensity of the opposition to gay marriage. Whatever any of us may think, they tell us, we can probably agree that the Bible has little to say about same-sex behavior, certainly much less than what it has to say about God's concern for justice, the poor, and caring for creation. Moreover, scholars are still debating the ambiguities and moral implications of those few texts that do deal with such behavior. If (here there's more disagreement) there are no powerful and irrefutable arguments against gay marriage, then, these people wonder, why are so many folks morally outraged by the very idea? What's the big deal? What explains all the passion that is tearing churches apart?

University of Virginia social psychologist Jonathan Haidt offers an answer.[47] Often, his research shows, the rationalist idea that we reason our way to moral judgments has it backwards. Instead, we make instant gut-level moral judgments and then seek rationalizations for our feelings. As the Scottish philosopher David Hume recognized long ago, reason is often the slave of passion. Moral reasoning aims to convince others of what we intuitively feel.

Thus, Haidt's studies show, many people will feel instant disgust over an objectively harmless but degrading behavior, such as scrubbing a toilet with the flag, and then will mentally scramble to construct moral reasons that support the moral intuition. First come the feelings, then the rationalization. Recent studies have similarly found that prejudice arises less from cerebral justifications than from automatic, gut-level reactions that seek justification.

If emotions feed moral intuitions, then we can appreciate both sides of the sex-war divide as occupied by morally concerned people. This is not an argument between moral and amoral people. "The two sides differ in their conceptions of the good," Haidt says, "not in the goodness of their motivations." Accepting this much is a first step toward calming hostilities and enabling a search for common ground, such as a shared interest in renewing marriage and enriching the flourishing that accompanies enduring human attachments.

Haidt's analysis also helps explain a phenomenon depicted in appendix B ("Attitudes are Changing"). Our attitudes about homosexuality arise not just from what we know but from *who* we know. Compared to those who don't knowingly know a gay person, those who do have a gay friend (and whose emotional responses to gay people are likely lessening) tend to express more acceptance of same-sex relationships.

The Bottom Line

Because marriage is inherently healthy, same-sex marriage will be healthier than its less permanent alternatives. It will likely not accelerate us down a slippery slope to promiscuity and polygamy. To the contrary, it has the potential to "let the air out of the tires of the alternatives-to-marriage movement."[48] It can prompt heterosexual men and women to appreciate marriage in a new way.

Sean Captain found that out while performing same-sex weddings as a deputized San Francisco marriage commissioner during the time when gay marriages were taking place there. He reported that he had "learned as much about love in a few days as I had in the previous 32 years." Observing tearful, joyous couples "strengthened my respect for the institution," he wrote. "It forced me to rethink the mild contempt I have had for marriage and realize how wonderful it can be when two people love each other so much that they are willing to tie their destinies together."[49]

Indeed, if implemented as part of a pro-marriage initiative, inviting gay couples to say "I do" may help reverse the growing tendency for straight couples to say "We don't."

Epilogue

In the very place where it was said to them, "You are not my people,"
there they shall be called children of the living God.

—Romans 9:26

IN A 2004 "FRIEND OF THE COURT" brief on behalf of seven
same-sex couples who were seeking full legal marriage rights in
New Jersey, the American Psychological Association emphasized
many of the same points we have made in this book. The brief,
offering a thorough review of the research literature, emphasized the benefits of marriage, the fact that "gay men and lesbians form stable, committed relationships that are equivalent
to heterosexual relationships in essential respects," and evidence
that "gay and lesbian parents are as fit and capable as heterosexual parents, and their children are as psychologically healthy and
well adjusted." But the organization also made another important point:

> By denying same-sex couples the right to marry, the state
> reinforces and perpetuates the stigma historically associated
> with homosexuality. . . . Stigma gives rise to prejudice, dis-
> crimination, and violence against people based on their sexual
> orientation. Research indicates that the experience of stigma
> and discrimination is associated with heightened psychologi-
> cal distress among gay men and lesbians. Being the target of
> extreme enactments of stigma, such as an antigay criminal
> assault, is associated with greater psychological distress than
> experiencing a similar crime not based on one's sexual orien-
> tation.[1]

A related point was made by church historian Martin Marty as he reflected on the 1998 murder of Matthew Shepherd, a young gay man in Wyoming. Marty likened today's homosexuals to the lepers of Jesus' day—people who were shunned by religious folk, but not by Jesus. "I believe that much antigay and anti-other activity is inspired by Christian rhetoric," he wrote. "But by now we must know that the attempt to love sinners while stirring hate about the sin, which after all, has to be done by those called sinners, contributes to the atmosphere in which crime occurs."[2]

By opening marriage to homosexual persons, society could go a long way toward removing the stigma that so many find painful to bear. In an essay that appeared on the Web site Beliefnet, the documentary filmmaker Macky Alston, son of a Presbyterian minister, tells of the psychological and spiritual healing he experienced in having a large church wedding, even though the ceremony was not legally recognized in the state in which he and his partner lived.

> Our wedding was like an exorcism. It cast out our shame and replaced it with the recognition that we are capable of loving, that we are loved by God and our community, and that our love is good and God-filled. We needed bells. We needed fanfare. We needed a cheering crowd. We needed a wedding. And that's what God delivered. . . . Perhaps more than anyone, I believe in the power of marriage to convert gay people from self-loathing to wellness, to being able to live and love the way God intends us to. But that's not all. Something happened that day at the altar. Nick and I are not the same. To put it into words is not possible. But take it from me: our love was blessed then and there by God in a new way. We were wed. Those whom God hath joined together let no one put asunder. This is my testimony.[3]

Christians in the "Muddled Middle"

Yet, for many people, the question of same-sex marriage is mind-blowing. Mark G. Toulouse, who teaches American religious history at Brite Divinity School, has written about the emergence of the "muddled middle," composed of "moderate liberals and evangelical moderates" who have gradually come to view sexual orientation as a neutral but "disordered" state and thus are able to support gay civil rights even though disapproving of homosexual practice. He believes that "muddling through is more hopeful than letting the language of culture wars control all future debates."[4] If "muddling through" means "encouraging continued discussion and debate in order to advance public understanding and create the proper environment for a careful and deliberative process," then so much the better.[5]

Toulouse sees at least four areas where differences emerge among the "muddled middle":

- *Contrasting approaches to the Bible.* "Those Christians who do not read the Bible literally are often muddled about knowing how to express its authority," he notes. In contrast, Christians who *do* read the Bible literally "seem to have no trouble muddling through an avoidance of its authority when they need to." They cherry-pick which verses should be applied, thereby condemning homosexuality while accepting divorce and remarriage. Toulouse says that part of the muddle for the middle is the lack of "hard consistencies in either the mainline or evangelical camps."[6]
- *Differences in how an ethics of sexuality is viewed.* Those leaning more toward the conservative side tend to emphasize rules regarding sexual *acts,* whereas those leaning more toward the liberal side are more concerned with *relationships.*
- *Different definitions of sexual sin.* "The more liberal middle emphasizes dehumanization as the culprit in sexual sin, while the more conservative side tends to emphasize sexual activity outside of marriage as the culprit," says Toulouse.[7]

- *Dissimilar uses of "nature" arguments.* Conservatives tend to use nature arguments to *oppose* homosexual practice (the sin-against-the-natural-order kind of emphasis), whereas liberals tend to use nature arguments to support committed same-sex relationships for persons whose nature (or natural orientation) is homosexual.

All of these views are part of the discussion we are encouraging in this book. We hope to reach out to Toulouse's "muddled middle" and keep the discussion going. We have empathy for our friends and colleagues who (unlike those on the fringe who loathe homosexuals) are good-hearted people who desire to be faithful to Scripture and supportive of marriage and who are concerned for the well-being of gays, but who have not come to the same conclusions as we have. If you fit that description, and if we haven't changed your mind, we hope at least to have engaged it.

Although changing our bedrock assumptions is never easy, the history of our ever-reforming church and culture is one of continual change. One thousand years ago most people *knew* that the earth was flat. Five hundred years ago, most people *knew* that the universe revolved around the earth. One hundred fifty years ago, most people *knew* that the earth was only a few thousand years old. Fifty years ago, most people *knew* (as did many fifty minutes ago) that sexual orientation was a moral choice.

Changing Win-Lose to Win-Win

In one of conflict researchers' favorite tales, a brother and sister quarreled over an orange. Finally they compromised and split the orange in half, whereupon the brother squeezed his half for juice while the sister used the peel from her half to make a cake. If only the siblings had agreed to split the orange by giving one all the juice and the other all the peel, their conflict could have been resolved to their mutual betterment.

Today's marriage war is a clash of those rightly concerned about marriage and the well-being of children versus those eager to encourage committed bonds and associated rights for gays and lesbians. Might it be possible to say that *both* are right, and thus for conservatives to get their juice and liberals their peel?

> Might liberals agree that, yes, marriage is conducive to health and well-being, and as a culture we should therefore resolve to do a much better job of supporting it, with marriage-friendly communal values, tax and corporate policies, and media models?
> Might conservatives agree that, yes, it's getting and keeping people married, not keeping gays *un*married, that really matters to us? Better to mandate the marriage option for all than to travel further down the road of alternatives to marriage.

The church is like a bird. It has a left wing and a right wing, and it flies best when combining the strength of both. Deuteronomy 32:11 compares God to a hovering mother eagle, stirring up her young, nudging them out of the safety of the nest to fly, and spreading her wings to catch and carry them if they begin to fall. Perhaps through our wrestling with same-sex marriage, God may be teaching the church to soar upward using both wings.

Might we then come together in honest, open dialogue? In small groups, might we engage one another in the spirit of Christ? Perhaps we can keep these thoughts in mind as we struggle to love one another and be receptive to God's will:

> When torn between judgment and grace, let us err on the side of grace.
> When torn between self-certain conviction and uncertain humility, let us err on the side of humility.
> When torn between contempt and love, let us err on the side of love.

In so doing, may we be more faithful disciples of the one who embodied grace, humility, and love in all he said and did. For "love is the fulfilling of the law" (Rom. 13:10).

Appendix A

Why Marriage Matters

Twenty-One Conclusions from the Social Sciences

A BIPARTISAN TEAM of family scholars chaired by Norval Glenn (University of Texas), Steven Nock (University of Virginia), and Linda Waite (University of Chicago) distilled evidence that indicates why "marriage is an important social good, associated with an impressively broad array of positive outcomes for children and adults alike."[*]

We preface their conclusions with three notes of caution: First, the social science findings reported here are *general patterns* and are not applicable to every individual situation. We can all think of cases that don't fit with most of the conclusions. Second, the findings convey no judgment toward persons who don't marry and who nevertheless may live very healthy, happy lives; the status of married and unmarried should not imply a hierarchical "caste" system, with those in one category deemed superior to those in the other. Third, the findings should not be read as fatalistic predictions that, for example, all children are likely to fail in school if their parents divorce or that all boys from single-parent homes will become juvenile delinquents (most such children do fine). Moreover, some marriages are toxic for family members.

Nevertheless, the team's findings[1] suggest that marriage has the following positive benefits:

---

[*] Statement sponsored by the Center of the American Experiment; the Coalition for Marriage, Family, and Couples Education; and the Institute for American Values (2002).

Family

1. Marriage increases the likelihood that fathers have good relationships with their children.
2. Cohabitation is not the functional equivalent of marriage.
3. Growing up outside an intact marriage increases the likelihood that children will themselves divorce or become unwed parents.
4. Marriage is a virtually universal human institution.

Economics

1. Divorce and unmarried childbearing increase poverty for both children and mothers.
2. Married couples seem to build more wealth on average than singles or cohabiting couples.
3. Married men earn more money than do single men with similar educational and job histories.
4. Parental divorce (or failure to marry) appears to increase children's risk of school failure.
5. Parental divorce reduces the likelihood that children will graduate from college and achieve high-status jobs.

Physical Health and Longevity

1. Children who live with their own two married parents enjoy better physical health, on average, than do children in other family forms.
2. Parental marriage is associated with a sharply lower risk of infant mortality.
3. Marriage is associated with reduced rates of alcohol and substance abuse for both adults and teens.
4. Married people, especially married men, have longer life expectancies than do otherwise similar singles.
5. Marriage is associated with better health and lower rates of injury, illness, and instability for both men and women.

Mental Health and Emotional Well-Being

1. Children whose parents divorce have higher rates of psychological distress and mental illness.

2. Divorce appears significantly to increase the risk of suicide . . . among both adults and adolescents.
3. Married mothers have lower rates of depression than do single or cohabiting mothers.

Crime and Domestic Violence

1. Boys raised in single-parent families are more likely to engage in delinquent and criminal behavior.
2. Marriage appears to reduce the risk that adults will be either perpetrators or victims of crime.
3. Married women appear to have a lower risk of experiencing domestic violence than do cohabiting or dating women.
4. A child who is not living with his or her own two married parents is at greater risk of child abuse.

Appendix B

Attitudes Are Changing

The dogmas of the quiet past are inadequate to the stormy present
. . . . so we must think anew, and act anew.
—Abraham Lincoln, State of the Union message, 1862

ATTITUDES ON IMPORTANT social issues sometimes, after much turmoil, do an about-face. Such a turnabout has happened to attitudes about race, gender, and even marriage. In 1951, for example, half of Americans advised parents who didn't get along to stay together for their children's sake. By 1994, only 15 percent agreed. By 2004, 66 percent of Americans were telling Gallup that divorce (for which people once were stigmatized) was "morally acceptable."

Opinion polls should not dictate ethics. When yesterday's majority opposed school desegregation, that did not make desegregation wrong. When today's majority—66 percent in a 2004 Gallup poll—judge gambling to be morally acceptable, that does not make gambling right. Right and wrong, conservatives and liberals agree, shouldn't be settled by an opinion poll. Ethics, including sexual ethics, must be decided on their own merits.

Still, we're wise to understand cultural trends and glimpse where things may be headed. And attitudes about sexual orientation are changing with remarkable speed.

Changing Attitudes About Homosexual Persons

First, support for equal employment rights for gays has risen to a near consensus:

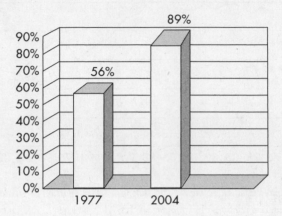

Fig. 3. Percent answering yes to the question "Should homosexuals have equal rights in terms of employment?" (Gallup)

Second, support for welcoming gays as teachers, armed forces officers, and even clergy has increased dramatically:

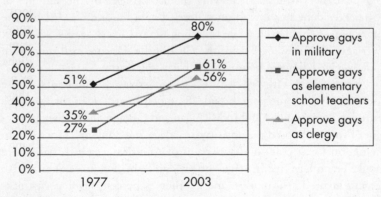

Fig. 4. Gallup surveys

Third, support for laws against same-sex relationships is plummeting:

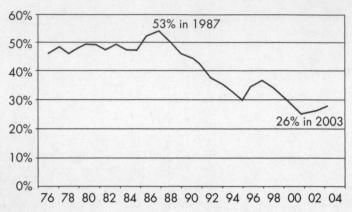

Fig. 5. Entering collegians agreeing with the statement "It is important to have laws prohibiting homosexual relationships" (annual UCLA/ACE surveys of 7 million entering collegians)

In the broader culture, the middle ground has shifted. Civil unions, a radical idea when the Vermont Legislature approved them in 2000, have become the moderate alternative—by granting some rights of marriage to gay partners while still denying them marriage. By the summer of 2004, President Bush, who once decried civil unions, was leaving the door open to them even while sounding the battle cry against same-sex marriages. In the week before the election he *supported* civil unions, in acknowledged disagreement with his party's platform.

After eleven states passed anti-gay-marriage amendments in the 2004 elections, some people said, "So much for the idea that people's attitudes are changing." But in Michigan and Oregon, more than 40 percent of voters opposed the anti-gay-marriage amendments. Moreover, in the national exit poll only 37 percent of Americans agreed that "there should be no legal recognition" of gay and lesbian couples. Thirty-five percent favored civil unions, and another 25 percent favored gay marriage. That makes it six in ten favoring either civil unions or marriage. In just four years, Vermont's "radical" initiative had become the moderate position.

Fourth, support for same-sex marriages is increasing (and is higher than 25 percent when "civil unions" aren't a possible alternative answer):

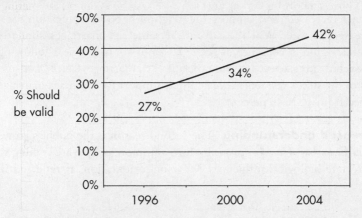

Fig. 6. "Do you think marriages between homosexuals should or should not be recognized by the law as valid?" (Gallup)

In Britain and Canada, a 2004 Gallup survey found half the population supporting gay marriage. The Supreme Court of Canada ruled in December 2004 that federal legislation to allow same-sex marriage throughout the country could proceed as a matter of equal rights under the constitution. Clergy, however, wouldn't be forced to officiate at same-sex marriages if they chose not to; their religious convictions would be protected under Canada's Charter of Rights and Freedoms. Just days before the Supreme Court of Canada's decision, the Supreme Court of Appeal in South Africa ruled that it was unconstitutional to exclude gays and lesbians from the definition of marriage, setting the stage for the legalization of same-sex marriage there, too. The Netherlands and Belgium have already opened marriage to same-sex couples.

Reasons for Changing Attitudes

We can expect that support for same-sex marriage will continue to increase, for four reasons:

Legislation and social practice One reason is that *attitudes tend to follow social practice.* Following the 1954 Supreme Court school-desegregation decision, the percentage of white Americans favoring integrated schools more than doubled and now includes nearly everyone. Likewise, following the Civil Rights Act of 1964, interracial contact increased, and support for neighborhood desegregation soon increased as well. Will the advent of same-sex marriages similarly engender more acceptance of such? It seems so. In the year following Massachussetts's 2004 adoption of same-sex marriage, *Boston Globe* surveys of the state's residents revealed that support for same-sex marriage surged from 40 to 56 percent.

Increased understanding The second reason is the public's growing *understanding of sexual orientation*. More and more people are coming to appreciate biological influences on sexual orientation, as reflected in figure 7:

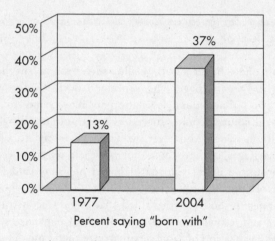

Fig. 7. "In your view, is homosexuality something a person is born with or is homosexuality due to other factors such as upbringing or environment?" (Gallup)

More personal acquaintance with gay and lesbian people
The third reason is that *gays have been coming out of the closet,* and, as the Christian gay activist (and former writer for Jerry Falwell, Billy Graham, and Pat Robertson) Mel White has said, what changes opinion is not so much "what you know about gay people, but that you know at least one gay person up close and personal."[1] Survey evidence is consistent with White's contention:

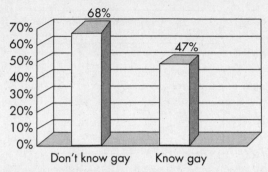

Fig. 8. Percent agreeing with the statement "Homosexual behavior is morally wrong" (Kaiser Family Foundation nation survey, 2000)

The growing visibility of gays and lesbians, in the media as well as in neighborhoods, workplaces, and schools, is self-compounding, notes essayist Adam Goodheart: "Each person who comes out of the closet brings at least some of his friends and family over to the pro-gay camp, and this in turn makes it easier for others to live openly."[2]

Generational change A final reason is *the changing of the generations.* The sad reality is that, as the old hymn says, "time, like an ever rolling stream, bears all who breathe away." Thus today's older Americans will soon no longer be with us, and today's younger Americans will take their place. Moreover, much research shows that attitudes and values laid down during the teen and early adult years tend to endure (which is one reason the church has no more important work than ministry to youth and young adults). And regarding attitudes toward same-sex marriage (and any other question pertaining to gay rights and relationships), the generation gap is profound:

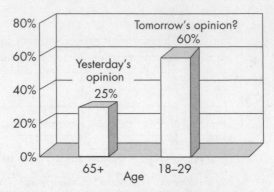

Fig. 9. Percent of Americans supporting gay and lesbian marriage (Kaiser Family Foundation national survey, 2000)

When today's older folks were yesterday's clear majority, we suffered no culture war over gay rights, same-sex marriage, or welcoming gays and lesbians into church membership and leadership. If the attitudes of today's young adults are sustained and become the attitudes of tomorrow's clear majority, we will enter a post-culture-war era. Today, in the in-between time of transition, we suffer the great divide.

Gender and Cultural Differences in Attitudes Toward Homosexuality

The divide is not only generational but also linked to gender and culture. No matter what the question, men are less accepting of gay rights and relationships than are women.

Culture is also a factor, both within and between countries. In the 2004 elections, opposition to the state anti-gay-marriage amendments ranged from 14 percent in Mississippi to 43 percent in Oregon. In Pew Research Center surveys taken in 2003, the culture gaps were even more enormous:

- The overwhelming majority of Africans (95 percent or more in Uganda, Nigeria, Mali, Senegal, and Kenya) said homosexuality should not "be accepted by society."
- South Americans were more evenly split, ranging from the 41 percent of Hondurans to the 66 percent of Argentineans who said that "homosexuality should be accepted by society."

- In North America, 51 percent of Americans said that "homosexuality should be accepted," as did 69 percent of Canadians.
- In Europe—the attitudinal opposite of Africa—support for acceptance of homosexuality ranged from 72 percent in Italy and 74 percent in Britain to 83 percent in Germany.

Small wonder that the worldwide Anglican Communion struggles to chart a path that can reconcile these radically divergent views of its geographically diverse constituents.

Numbers, we all agree, should not decide ethics. But as neuroscience and psychology document the natural basis for sexual orientation and its resistance to change, as students become educated regarding these findings, as more and more gays and lesbians become known to friends and family members, and as generational turnover rolls in as inexorably as an ocean tide, it's pretty clear where things are headed.

How Should the Church Respond?

As we have seen throughout this book, religion influences how people view homosexual behavior. This becomes clear in surveys in which religious affiliation is taken into account:

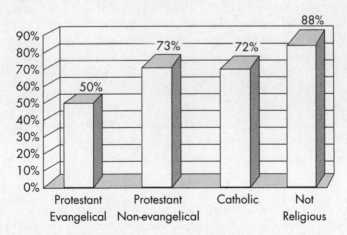

Fig. 10. Percent agreeing with the statement "Homosexuality is a normal part of some people's sexuality" (Kaiser Family Foundation national survey, 2000)

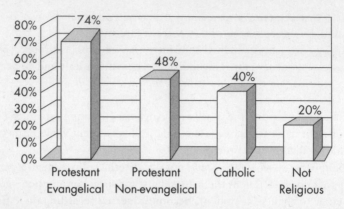

Fig. 11. Percent agreeing with the statement "Homosexual behavior is morally wrong" (Kaiser Family Foundation national survey, 2000)

That leaves us to ponder: Is the conservative church to be commended for sandbagging against the oncoming tide of support for gay aspirations (much as we commend turning back the corrosive tide of individualism, nonmarital childbearing, fleeting sexual "hook-ups," and the media modeling of impulsive sexuality)? Or is it handcuffing the faith to railroad tracks on which an unstoppable train is bearing down?

This much seems to be historical fact: people of faith have repeatedly debated and then changed their minds regarding marital ethics, moving

- from favoring arranged marriages to expecting romantic choice;
- from viewing marriage as inferior to celibacy (though "better to marry than to be aflame with passion") to seeing it as an equal calling;
- from assuming male headship to welcoming marital mutuality;
- from stigmatizing interracial marriage to accepting it;
- from disciplining divorced people in faith communities to embracing them.

In each case, our Christian ancestors have found proof texts to support their assumptions. Black people, the Scriptures once seemed to say, were the accursed descendants of Noah's son Ham, and not suited for marriage with white people. Wives were to submit to their husbands "as to the Lord." Are we in the midst of one more such change? Will our great-grandchildren look back on today's sex war as but another chapter in the church's ever-reforming history?

Rethinking topics we thought were already settled is never easy. We humans like certainty and order, and we're already reeling from the rapid pace of change in so many areas of modern life. Asking that we reexamine long-held beliefs about something as basic as marriage and sexuality may be extremely stressful—even threatening. We might even be afraid that, by reexamining our theological understanding in view of scientific findings and changing social attitudes, we are somehow betraying God. Some of us may therefore avoid asking new questions about biblical interpretation, choosing instead to stay in the comfort zone of a belief that all the answers are already in.

Our sense of self, of who we are as believers, is deeply tied to what we understand about who God is, what God's purpose is for human beings, how we can know God's will, and what it means to love, serve, and obey God. Changes in any aspect of such understanding do not come readily and may cause us, as individuals, deep emotional anguish at our very core. As we have already seen, the early Christians found that out in their inner and outer struggles over circumcision, dietary rules, and special holy days. But a look at history shows us that the world is *not* stagnant. Things don't remain the same, no matter where we look. Life happens, time passes, attitudes are in flux, and changes do occur. The question is, how do we wish to respond to the challenges those changes entail?

Appendix C

Discussion Questions

Chapter 1. The Great Divide

1. Why is the debate over gay marriage considered an example of a "culture war"? How would you describe each of the cultures involved in this great divide? Suggest some possible reasons for the clash.

2. What do some people believe will happen if same-sex marriage is legalized?

3. On page 7, the authors describe the life of faith as "a dance on the boundary between conviction and humility." Tell why you agree or disagree.

4. Do you agree that both biblical and natural revelation point to God's truth? What priority does each deserve? Are these the only ways we can learn about God?

Chapter 2. The Longing for Belonging

1. If a person feels rejected or ignored, what are some ways he or she might react?

2. Do you agree or disagree with the authors' comments about a link between depression and the Western emphasis on individualism? Explain your answer.

3. What are four important factors in the pursuit of happiness? Think of ways in which you have found any or all of them to be important in your own pursuit of happiness.

4. What are some possible reasons for the correlation between happiness and marriage? Between health and marriage? Do you believe that these same correlations would be found in marriages in which both partners were of the same sex?

5. The authors say that "we find we're most 'real' in connectedness to others." Can you think of specific times when you have found this to be true in your own life?

Chapter 3. The State of Our Unions

1. What is marriage, and how does it differ from other relationships?
2. On page 25, the author of a book on singleness is quoted as saying that the happiness experienced by many single persons is "different than mated happiness, but it is still happiness." What do you think she meant?
3. What do you think about the argument that having more choices often leads to less happiness?
4. What are some possible reasons that the risk of a future divorce is greater for persons who have cohabited than for those who have not? What is the one possible exception found in new data?
5. Why do some people believe that gay and lesbian couples should not be allowed to marry, even though the data clearly show that the institution of marriage is good for people, for children, and for society?

Chapter 4. A Newer World

1. What are three toxic forces that are challenging marriage and family life today?
2. What are some ways that a society's economic system affects families?
3. Can you give specific examples of violence and sexual behavior portrayed in television programs, movies, and video games that may be expected to impact viewers in the ways listed on pages 44–45?
4. Do you agree or disagree that the actions and events listed on pages 49–50 are signs of a desire for a more family-supporting world? What factors might hinder such changes?

Chapter 5. Understanding Sexual Orientation

1. What assumptions are behind the wording of such questions as "What causes left-handedness" or "What causes homosexuality"? Why do researchers instead study *handedness* in general or seek to understand *sexual orientation* in the broadest sense?
2. In attempting to understand sexual orientation, why is it important for followers of Jesus to keep in mind certain basics of our faith that we hold in common?

3. In recent years, scientific studies, greater openness to discussion, denominational task forces, and extensive media coverage have helped increase the understanding of sexual orientation among persons of faith. In approaching the topic, what are some areas of agreement today? What are two main areas of disagreement about sexual orientation?

4. Tell why you believe that sexual orientation is or is not a choice.

5. To what extent might environment, including parental influence, affect a person's sexual orientation?

6. To what extent does biology likely play a part in sexual orientation?

Chapter 6. Changing Sexual Orientation

1. What are some things we human beings can change about ourselves? What are some things we can't change?

2. What is reparative therapy? What are two assumptions underlying reparative therapy? What do the major American mental health organizations say about reparative therapy?

3. What would you say to a homosexual friend or relative who yearns to change his or her sexual orientation? What would you say to a homosexual friend or relative who has no desire to change and who, in fact, feels that his or her homosexuality is a gift from God?

4. Do you think the hypothetical experiment described on page 82 could be carried out? Do you believe it would supply definitive answers to the question of changing sexual orientation? Why or why not?

Chapter 7. What the Bible Does and Doesn't Say

1. What Scripture texts are most frequently cited in discussions of same-sex sexual acts? Why is it so important to notice the context in which these passages appear?

2. If Scripture is its own best commentary, what do we know about the reasons God judged Sodom so harshly?

3. What are some of the behaviors to which the word *abomination* is applied in Scripture? Have you ever heard anyone apply the word to any of these behaviors? Why do you think that people are so quick to apply the word only to same-sex sexual acts and not to anything else?

4. What does the Bible say was the reason that God gave the holiness code to ancient Israel?

5. How have various translations of Scripture contributed to negative attitudes toward gay and lesbian persons?

6. Compare today's struggles over homosexuality with the struggles of the early church over the religious rite of circumcision, the observance of special holy days, and dietary rules. In what sense were these disputes also "culture wars"?

Chapter 8. What God Has Joined Together?

1. What are some possible reasons that deeply felt religious fervor fuels many of the legal challenges to gay marriage?

2. What is the one difference in the two paradigms describing the characteristics of marriage? How important do you believe this difference to be?

3. Why do some Christians believe it is important to view gender as complementarity. How do they apply this view to questions about God's intent in creating sexuality?

4. Do you believe that biblical teachings about marriage allow for the possibility of two same-sex persons forming such a relationship? Why or why not?

5. In what sense might a homosexual person consider his or her sexual orientation as a burden? As a blessing? What might make the difference?

6. How does excluding gay people from marriage stigmatize who they are and whom they love? Try to think of specific examples that you have read about or may know about personally.

Chapter 9. Gay Marriage

1. Why do some people believe that the legalization of gay marriage would be destructive to the institution of the family?

2. How might same-sex marriage be beneficial not only to the partners but to society?

3. What are some common arguments against same-sex marriage?

4. Why is asking for "equal rights" for gay and lesbian people *not* the same as asking for "special rights," as is sometimes charged?

5. Why or why not might civil unions for gay and lesbian people be a solution to the debates about legalizing same-sex marriage?

6. What are some ways the institution of marriage has changed over history?

7. What is known about gay parenting and its effects on children?
8. Why do some people feel that heterosexual marriage must be "defended" from the entrance of gays into the institution?
9. How might the legalization of gay marriage halt trends toward "marriage lite" alternatives?

Epilogue

1. What is the relationship between the stigmatization of homosexuality and violence against gays and lesbians?
2. What does Mark Toulouse mean when he says that a large proportion of people within the religious community belong to the "muddled middle" when it comes to questions of homosexuality and gay marriage?
3. What, according to Toulouse, are the two different ways an ethics of sexuality is viewed by Christians leaning toward one side of the divide or the other?
4. What are the main differences of opinion about what constitutes sexual sin?
5. What are the contrasting ways in which "nature" arguments are used by those open to gay marriage and those opposed to it?
6. Why are grace, humility, and love essential elements in discussions of same-sex marriage?

Notes

Chapter 1: The Great Divide

1. Story told Martin E. Marty in his newsletter, *Sightings*, June 11, 2001.
2. Wesley Granberg-Michaelsen in an address to the General Synod meeting of the Reformed Church in America, 1998).
3. James Dobson, "In Defending Marriage: Take the Offensive," *Dr. Dobson's Newsletter*, April 2004, http://www.family.org/docstudy/newsletters/a0031315.cfm.
4. Charles Colson, "Urgent Memo [to] All Breakpoint Supporters," December 2003.
5. Charles Colson, "Doing Your Own Thing: Why Same-Sex 'Marriage' Undermines Family Stability," *BreakPoint*, November 26, 2003, http://www.leaderu.com/socialsciences/colson-gaymarr-compendium.html.
6. "Pope: Same-Sex Unions 'Degrade' Marriage" (*Boston Globe*/Associated Press, February 29, 2004).
7. Congregation for the Doctrine of the Faith, "Considerations Regarding Proposals to Give Legal Recognition to Unions Between Homosexual Persons," http://www.vatican.va/.
8. Bob Herbert, "Bliss and Bigotry," *New York Times*, February 27, 2004, http://www.nytimes.com/.
9. Dino Georgiou, letter to the editor, *New York Times*, February 6, 2004, http://www.nytimes.com/.
10. Data taken from *The American Freshman*, compiled from an annual survey conducted by UCLA and the American Council of Education, available at www.gseis.ucla.edu/heri/heri.html. For more on social trends, see app. B, "Attitudes Are Changing."
11. Dobson, "In Defending Marriage."
12. Andrew Sullivan, "Integration Day," *New York Times*, May 17, 2004, http://www.nytimes.com/.
13. Dobson, "In Defending Marriage."
14. "The Marriage Movement: A Statement of Principles," *Marriage Movement.org*, June 2000, http://www.marriagemovement.org/.

Chapter 2: The Longing for Belonging

1. Roy Baumeister and Mark Leary, "The Need to Belong: Desire for Interpersonal Attachment as a Fundamental Human Motivation," *Psychological Bulletin* 117 (1995): 497–529.
2. Ellen Berscheid, "Interpersonal Attraction," in *The Handbook of Social Psychology,* ed. G. Lindzey and E. Aronson (New York: Random House, 1985).
3. M. R. Leary, A. L. Haupt, K. S. Strausser, and J. T. Chokel, "Calibrating the Sociometer: The Relationship Between Interpersonal Appraisals and State Self-Esteem," *Journal of Personality and Social Psychology* 74 (1998): 1290–99.
4. Kipling D. Williams, *Ostracism: The Power of Silence* (New York: Guilford, 2002).
5. J. M. Twenge, R. F. Baumeister, D. M. Tice, and T. S. Stucke, "If You Can't Join Them, Beat Them: Effects of Social Exclusion on Aggressive Behavior," *Journal of Personality and Social Psychology* 81 (2001): 1058–69; J. M. Twenge, K. R. Catanese, and R. F. Baumeister, "Social Exclusion Causes Self-Defeating Behavior," *Journal of Personality and Social Psychology* 83 (2002): 606–15; R. F. Baumeister, J. M. Twenge, and C. K. Nuss, "Effects of Social Exclusion on Cognitive Processes: Anticipated Aloneness Reduces Intelligent Thought," *Journal of Personality and Social Psychology* 83 (2002): 817–27.
6. S. Bowles and M. Kasindorf, "Friends Tell of Picked-on but 'Normal' Kid," *USA Today,* March 6, 2001, 4A.
7. Martin Seligman, *Learned Optimism* (New York: Knopf, 1991). See also Ed Diener and Martin Seligman, "Beyond Money: Toward an Economy of Well-Being," *Psychological Science in the Public Interest* 5 (2004): 1–31.
8. John Bowlby, *Attachment and Loss,* vol. 3, *Loss: Sadness and Depression* (London: Basic Books, 1980).
9. David G. Myers, *The Pursuit of Happiness* (New York: Morrow, 1992; Avon, 1993).
10. Diener and Seligman, "Beyond Money."
11. General Social Survey data analyzed by David Myers from data archives online from the University of California.
12. Arne Mastekaasa, "Age Variations in the Suicide Rates and Self-Reported Subjective Well-Being of Married and Never Married Persons," *Journal of Community and Applied Social Psychology* 5 (1995), 21–39.
13. Letitia Anne Peplau and Kristin P. Beals, "The Family Lives of Lesbians and Gay Men," in *Handbook of Family Communication,* ed. A. L. Vangelisti (Mahwah, NJ: Erlbaum, 2003).
14. Lawrence A. Kurdek, "Are Gay and Lesbian Cohabiting Couples *Really* Different from Heterosexual Married Couples?" *Journal of Marriage and Family* (in press).

15. Janet Lever, "Sexual Revelations," *Advocate*, August 1994, 17, 24.

16. David summarizes pertinent research in David Myers, *Psychology*, 7th ed. (New York: Worth Publishers, 2004), as does Shelley Taylor in *Positive Illusions: Creative Self-Deception and the Healthy Mind* (New York: Basic Books, 1991).

17. G. E. Vaillant, *Aging Well: Surprising Guideposts to a Happier Life from the Landmark Harvard Study of Adult Development* (Boston: Little, Brown, 2002).

18. J. E. Murray, "Marital Protection and Marital Selection: Evidence from a Historical-Prospective Sample of American Men," *Demography* 37 (2000), 511–21.

19. C. M. Wilson and A. J. Oswald, "How Does Marriage Affect Physical and Psychological Health? A Survey of the Longitudinal Evidence" (working paper, Univ. of York and Warwick Univ., UK, 2002).

20. J. K. Kiecolt-Glaser and T. L. Newton, "Marriage and Health: His and Hers," *Psychological Bulletin* 127 (2001): 472–503.

21. H. E. Marano, "Debunking the Marriage Myth: It Works for Women, Too" *New York Times*, August 4,1998, http://www.nytimes.com/.

22. P. M. Eng, I. Kawachi, G. Fitzmaurice, and E. B. Rimm, "Effects of Marital Transitions on Changes in Dietary and Other Health Behaviors in Men" (paper presented at the American Psychosomatic Society meeting, 2001).

23. Eccles. 4:10.

24. S. Cohen, W. J. Doyle, D. P. Skoner, B. S. Rabin and J. M. Gwaltney Jr., "Social Ties and Susceptibility to the Common Cold," *Journal of the American Medical Association* 277 (1997): 1940–44.

25. B. N. Uchino, J. T. Cacioppo, and J. K. Kiecolt-Glaser, "The Relationship Between Social Support and Physiological Processes: A Review with Emphasis on Underlying Mechanisms and Implications for Health," *Psychological Bulletin* 119 (1996): 488–531; B. N. Uchino, D. Uno, and J. Holt-Lunstad, "Social Support, Physiological Processes, and Health," *Current Directions in Psychological Science* 8 (1999): 145–48.

26. J. Pennebaker, *Opening Up: The Healing Power of Confiding in Others* (New York: William Morrow, 1990); J. W. Pennebaker, S. D. Barger, and J. Tiebout, "Disclosure of Traumas and Health Among Holocaust Survivors," *Psychosomatic Medicine* 51 (1989): 577—89; J. W. Pennebaker and R. C. O'Heeron, "Confiding in Others and Illness Rate Among Spouses of Suicide and Accidental Death Victims," *Journal of Abnormal Psychology* 93 (1984): 473–76.

27. C. S. Lewis, "Membership," in *The Weight of Glory and Other Addresses* (New York: Macmillan, 1949).

28. Diener and Seligman, "Beyond Money."

29. Margery Williams, *The Velveteen Rabbit; or, How Toys Become Real* (Garden City, NY: Doubleday, 1926).

30. Desmond Tutu: *No Future Without Forgiveness* (New York: Doubleday, 1999).

Chapter 3: The State of Our Unions

1. Lydia Saad, "Democrats and Republicans Agree That U.S. Morals Are Subpar," Gallup Poll News Service, May 21, 2004, http://www.gallup.com/.

2. Quoted in Martin Miller, "Unattached, Thank You, and Loving It," *Los Angeles Times,* September 2, 2004.

3. L. J. Sax, S. Hurtado, J. A. Lindholm, A. W. Astin, W. S. Korn, and K. M. Mahoney, *The American Freshman: National Norms for Fall 2004* (Los Angeles: Higher Education Research Institute, UCLA, 2004).

4. "Marriage: Mix and Match," *New York Times,* March 3, 2004.

5. Quoted in Karla B. Hackstaff, "The Rise of Divorce Culture and Its Gendered Foundations," *Feminism and Psychology* 3 (1993): 363–68.

6. *America's Adults and Teens Sound Off About Teen Pregnancy: An Annual National Survey* (Washington, DC: National Campaign to Prevent Teen Pregnancy, 2003).

7. These data can be harvested from the National Opinion Research Center's General Social Survey archive. See also Norval Glenn, "The Social and Cultural Meaning of Contemporary Marriage," in *The Retreat from Marriage,* ed. Bryce Christensen (Rockford, IL: The Rockford Institute, 1990); Norval Glenn, "The Course of Marital Success and Failure in Five American 10-Year Marriage Cohorts," *Journal of Marriage and the Family* 60 (1998): 569–76; Robert E. Lane, "Searching for Lost Companions in the Groves of the Market" (paper presented at the conference "Understanding Quality of Life: Enjoyment and Suffering," Princeton, NJ, November 1996); and Stacy J. Rogers and Paul R. Amato, "Is Marital Quality Declining? The Evidence from Two Generations," *Social Forces* 75 (1997): 1089–1100.

8. *Monitoring the Future Survey* (Institute for Social Research, Univ. of Michigan, 2004).

9. Linda Lyons, "How Many Teens Are Cool with Cohabitation?" *Gallup Poll Tuesday Briefing,* April 13, 2004.

10. Thanks to Barbara Dafoe Whitehead for this analogy.

11. Elizabeth Taylor, quoted in *Time,* October 20, 1997, 21.

12. For detailed citations, see David G. Myers, *The American Paradox: Spiritual Hunger in an Age of Plenty* (New Haven: Yale Univ. Press, 2000).

13. David Popenoe and Barbara Dafoe Whitehead, *The State of Our Unions, 2004* (Piscatawah, NJ: The National Marriage Project, Rutgers Univ., 2004), 21. The study to which they refer is Jay Teachman, "Premarital Sex, Premarital Cohabitation, and the Risk of Subsequent Matial Disruption Among Women," *Journal of Marriage and the Family* 65 (2003): 444–55. For more on pre- vs. postengagement cohabitation, see Galena H. Kline, Scott M. Stanley, Howard J. Markman, P. Antonio Olmos-Gallo, Michelle St. Peters, Sara W. Whitton, and Lydia M. Prado, "Timing Is Everything: Pre-engagement

Cohabitation and Increased Risk for Poor Marital Outcomes," *Journal of Family Psychology* 18 (2004): 311–18.

14. Renata Forste and Koray Tanfer, "Sexual Exclusivity Among Dating, Cohabiting and Married Women," *Journal of Marriage and the Family* 58 (1996): 33–47. The result comes from young adult women only (surveyed in the 1991 National Survey of Women).

15. William G. Axinn and Jennifer S. Barber, "Living Arrangements and Family Formation Attitudes in Early Adulthood," *Journal of Marriage and the Family* 59 (1997): 595–611.

16. "Couples Who Give Their Marriage a Lower Grade—That Is, B or Below—Are More Likely to Say They Lived Together Before Marriage Than Are Those Who Give Their Marriage an A," *Gallup Poll Monthly,* September 1996, 19.

17. Brad Edmondson, "New Lifestage: Trial Marriage," *Forecast,* October 1997, http://www.demographics.com/publications/fc/97_fc/9710_fc/fc07106.htm. Edmondson uses data from the National Center for Health Statistics.

18. See David Popenoe and Barbara Dafoe Whitehead, *Should We Live Together? What Young Adults Need to Know About Cohabitation Before Marriage: A Comprehensive Review of Recent Research* (Piscataway, NJ: National Marriage Project, 2002).

19. Linda J. Waite, "Cohabitation: A Communitarian Perspective," *Communitarian Network* (Washington, D.C.), 1999. See also Linda J. Waite and Maggie Gallagher, *The Case for Marriage* (Cambridge, MA: Harvard Univ. Press, 2000). The U.S. domestic violence data were analyzed by Waite from the 1987–88 National Survey of Families and Households.

20. Maggie Gallagher, *The Abolition of Marriage* (Washington, DC: Regnery Publishing, 1996), 167–68.

21. Patrick T. Davies and E. Mark Cummings, "Marital Conflict and Child Adjustment: An Emotional Security Hypothesis," *Psychological Bulletin* 116 (1994): 387–411.

22. Paul R. Amato and Alan Booth, *A Generation at Risk: Growing Up in an Era of Family Upheaval* (Cambridge, MA: Harvard Univ. Press, 1997).

23. Seligman, *Learned Optimism,* 146–47.

24. E. Mavis Hetherington, "Marriage and Divorce American Style: A Destructive Marriage Is Not a Happy Family," *American Prospect,* April 8, 2002, http://www.prospect.org/.

25. Behavior geneticists remind us that biological parents and their children share genes. For example, compared with men who propagate and stay, those who propagate and split may be more impulsive (and therefore crime-prone)—and so may the children who carry their genes. Genetics cannot, however, account for the joint decline of both marriage and child well-being between 1960 and the early 1990s. Cultures can change quickly; genes cannot.

26. See Judith Rich Harris, *The Nurture Assumption* (New York: Free Press, 1998).

27. See www.unmarried.org.

28. Sara McLanahan and Gary Sandefur, *Growing Up with a Single Parent* (Cambridge, MA: Harvard Univ. Press, 1994), 10.

29. William Galston, "A Liberal-Democratic Case for the Two-Parent Family," *Responsive Community* 1 (1990–1991): 14–26.

30. Molly Ivins, Creators Syndicate column, *Grand Rapids Press*, September 11, 1995, A10.

31. Credit for the hurricane analogy is due to Barbara Dafoe Whitehead's classic article "Dan Quayle Was Right," *Atlantic*, April 1993, 47–84.

32. Nicholas Zill, "Behavior, Achievement, and Health Problems Among Children in Stepfamilies: Findings from a National Survey of Child Health," in *Impact of Divorce, Single Parenting, and Stepparenting on Children*, ed. E. Mavis Hetherington and Josephine D. Arasteh (Hillsdale, NJ: Erlbaum, 1988). The 1988 survey is summarized in a 1991 report by Deborah A. Dawson, "Family Structure and Children's Health: United States, 1988," in *Vital and Health Statistics, Series 10: Data from the National Health Survey, no. 178* (Hyattsville, MD: National Center for Statistics, U.S. Department of Health and Human Services, DHHS Publication no. PHS 91–1506).

33. James L. Peterson and Nicholas Zill, "Marital Disruption, Parent-Child Relationships, and Behavior Problems in Children," *Journal of Marriage and the Family* 48 (1986): 295–307.

34. Andrew J. Cherlin, et. al., "Longitudinal Studies of Effects of Divorce on Children in Great Britain and the United States," *Science* 252 (1991): 1386–89.

35. Pepper Schwartz, "When Staying Is Worth the Pain," *New York Times*, April 4, 1995, C1, quoted in David Popenoe, *Life Without Father* (New York: Free Press, 1996), 209.

36. Andrew J. Cherlin, Kathleen E. Kiernan, and P. Lindsay Chase-Lansdale, "Parental Divorce in Childhood and Demographic Outcomes in Young Adulthood," *Demography* 32 (1995): 299–316.

37. Andrew J. Cherlin, P. Lindsay Chase-Lansdale, and Christine McRae, "Effects of Parental Divorce on Mental Health Throughout the Life Course," *American Sociological Review* 63 (1998): 239–49.

38. P. Lindsay Chase-Lansdale, Andrew J. Cherlin, and Kathleen E. Kiernan, "The Long-Term Effects of Parental Divorce on the Mental Health of Young Adults: A Developmental Perspective," *Child Development* 66 (1995): 1614–34.

39. Quoted in Whitehead, "Dan Quayle Was Right."

40. James Dobson, "The Battle for Marriage," webcast from Colorado Springs New Life Church, May 23, 2004, http://www.dvstudios.com/ccn/frc_webcast.html.

41. K. A. Moore, S. M. Jekielek, and C. Emig, "Marriage from a Child's Perspective: How Does Family Structure Affect Children, and What Can We Do

About It?" Washington, DC: Child Trends Research Brief, 2002, http://www.childtrends.org/.

42. Ellen Goodman, Washington Post's Writers Group, March 16, 1993.

Chapter 4: A Newer World

1. Paul Krugman, "Turn of the Century," *New York Times*, June 18, 2000, http://www.nytimes.com/.
2. William Julius Wilson, *When Work Disappears: The World of the New Urban Poor* (New York: Knopf, 1996).
3. Quoted in Mitchell Landsberg, "Benton Harbor Leads Single Parent Parade," Associated Press, *Grand Rapids Press*, September 19, 1994.
4. Quoted in Doug Bandow, "Can 'Unbridled Capitalism' Be Tamed?" *Wall Street Journal*, March 19, 1997.
5. Bryce Christensen, "Far More Than a Health Club: How the Family Guards Health and Alleviates Sickness," *Family in America*, April 1998, 1–7.
6. Quoted in Don Eberly, *Restoring the Good Society: A New Vision for Politics and Culture* (Grand Rapids, MI: Baker Books, 1994), 61–62, taken from Mark C. Henrie, "Rethinking American Conservatism in the 1990s: The Struggle Against Homogenization," *Intercollegiate Review*, spring 1993, 14.
7. Quoted in Fred M. Hechinger, "About Education," *New York Times*, February 28, 1990, 1.
8. Russell Kirk, *The Politics of Prudence* (Bryn Mawr, PA: Intercollegiate Studies Institute, 1993), 30, quoted in Eberly, *Restoring the Good Society*, 62.
9. Ed Donnerstein, "Why Do We Have Those Ratings on Television" (address to the National Institute on the Teaching of Psychology, St. Petersburg Beach, FL, 1998).
10. George Lucas, remarks at Academy Award ceremonies, 1992.
11. For more detailed sources for media watching and influence findings, see David G. Myers, *Social Psychology*, 8th ed. (New York: McGraw-Hill, 2005).
12. American Psychological Association, "Violence in the Media," http://www.psychologymatters.org/mediaviolence.html.
13. American Psychiatric Association, "Psychiatric Effects of Media Violence," http://www.psych.org/public_info/media_violence.cfm.
14. For a summary of these findings, see Myers, *Social Psychology*.
15. Edward Donnerstein, Daniel Linz, and Steven Penrod, *The Question of Pornography* (New York: Free Press, 1987).
16. Quoted in Judy Blume, "The First Lady Talks TV," *TV Guide*, November 13, 1993, 12.
17. C. Everett Koop, "Report of the Surgeon General's Workshop on Pornography and Public Health," *American Psychologist* 42 (1987): 944–45. For more information

on the mixed evidence regarding rape myths, see Mike Allen, Tara Emmers, Lisa Gebhardt, and Mary Giery, "Exposure to Pornography and Acceptance of Rape Myths," *Journal of Communication* 45 (1995): 5–26.

18. Adam Nagourney and Janet Elder, "Americans Show Clear Concern on Bush Agenda," *New York Times*, November 23, 2004, http://www.nytimes.com/.

19. Ellen Goodman, "Hollywood Needs to Reel In Higher Quality," *Washington Post Writers Group* column appearing in the *Grand Rapids Press*, 1995.

20. William Galston, "A Liberal-Democratic Case for the Two-Parent Family," *The Responsive Community*, winter 1990–1991, 14–26.

21. Quoted in Sharon Waxman, "Study Finds Film Ratings Are Growing More Lenient," *New York Times*, July 14, 2004.

22. http://www.scenesmoking.org/.

23. Gloria Steinem, "Six Great Ideas That Television Is Missing," in *Public Communication and Behavior*, ed. George Comstock (New York: Academic Press, 1988).

24. William Bennett and DeLores Tucker Story recounted by William Bennett at the 1995 White House Conference on Character Building for Democratic Civil Society. See also Sonya Ross, "Hip-Hopping Mad: Crusader Targets Gangsta' Rap," Associated Press, *Grand Rapids Press*, September 5, 1995, C1, C2; and Robert Peters, "Time Warner Still in the Porn Business," *Morality in Media*, September–October 1998, 3–4. Lyrics from ESham's song "Ex-Girlfriend."

25. Edward Donnerstein, Daniel Linz, and Steven Penrod, *The Question of Pornography* (London: Free Press, 1987), 196.

26. High school seniors survey Monitoring the Future surveys, conducted by the University of Michigan's Survey Research Center.

27. As reported in National Marriage Project, *State of Our Unions* (TK: Rutgers Univ., 2004).

28. The document is available online at http://marriage.rutgers.edu/.

Chapter 5: Understanding Sexual Orientation

1. T. G. M. Sandfort, R. de Graaf, R. Bijl, and P. Schnabel, "Same-Sex Sexual Behavior and Psychiatric Disorders," *Archives of General Psychiatry* 58 (2001): 85–91.

2. http://sda.berkeley.edu:7502 (search for data from "sexsex" question).

3. Tom W. Smith, *American Sexual Behavior: Trends, Socio-Demographic Differences, and Risk Behavior*, GSS Topical Report no. 25 (Chicago: National Opinion Research Center, Univ. of Chicago, 2003), 7–8.

4. Anthony F. Bogaert, "Asexuality: Prevalence and Associated Factors in a National Probability Sample," *Journal of Sex Research* 41 (2004): 279–287.

5. Quoted in Thomas Crampton, "Using the Courts to Wage a War on Gay Marriage," *New York Times*, May 9, 2004, http://www.nytimes.com/.

6. Quoted in Letha Dawson Scanzoni, "Can Homosexuals Change?" *The Other Side,* January 1984, 14.

7. A. P. Bell, M. S. Weinberg, and S. K. Hammersmith, *Sexual Preference: Its Development in Men and Women* (Bloomington: Indiana Univ. Press, 1981); S. K. Hammersmith, "Sexual Preference: An Empirical Study from the Alfred C. Kinsey Institute for Sex Research" (paper presented at the meeting of the American Psychological Association, Washington, DC, August 1982).

8. A. M. Ludwig, *The Price of Greatness: Resolving the Creativity and Madness Controversy* (New York: Guilford Press, 1995).

9. D. Binson, S. Michaels, R. Stall, T. J. Coates, J. H. Gagnon, and J. A. Catania, "Prevalence and Social Distribution of Men Who Have Sex with Men: United States and Its Urban Centers," *Journal of Sex Research* 32 (1995): 245–54; E. O. Laumann, J. H. Gagnon, R. T. Michael, and S. Michaels, *The Social Organization of Sexuality: Sexual Practices in the United States* (Chicago: Univ. of Chicago Press, 1994).

10. A. Tarmann, "Out of the Closet and onto the Census Long Form," *Population Today* 30 (May–June 2002): 1, 6.

11. M. D. Storms, "A Theory of Erotic Orientation Development," *Psychological Review* 88 (1981): 340–53.

12. A. F. Bogaert, C. Friesen, and P. Klentrou, "Age of Puberty and Sexual Orientation in a National Probability Sample," *Archives of Sexual Behavior* 31 (2002): 73–81.

13. J. Money, "Sin, Sickness, or Status? Homosexual Gender Identity and Psychoneuroendocrinology," *American Psychologist* 42 (1987): 384–99.

14. D. J. Bem, "Exotic Becomes Erotic: A Developmental Theory of Sexual Orientation," *Psychological Review* 103 (1996): 320–35; Bem, "Exotic Becomes Erotic: Interpreting the Biological Correlates of Sexual Orientation," *Archives of Sexual Behavior* 29 (2000): 531–48.

15. Scott Hershberger, "Biological Factors in the Development of Sexual Orientation," in *Lesbian, Gay, and Bisexual Identities and Youth: Psychological Perspectives,* ed. A. R. D'Augelli and C. J. Patterson (New York: Oxford Univ. Press, 2001), 27–51. See also Qazi Rahman and Glenn D. Wilson, "Born Gay? The Psychobiology of Human Sexual Orientation," *Personality and Individual Differences* 34 (2003): 1337–82; and Glenn D. Wilson and Qazi Rahman, *Born Gay: The Biology of Sexual Orientation* (London: Peter Owne, 2005).

16. Bruce Bagemihl, *Biological Exuberance: Animal Homosexuality and Natural Diversity* (New York: St. Martins, 1999). See also Joan Roughgarden, *Evolution's Rainbow: Diversity, Gender, and Sexuality in Nature and People* (Berkeley: Univ. of California Press, 2004).

17. See, for example, Anne Perkins and James A. Fitzgerald, "Sexual Orientation in Domestic Rams: Some Biological and Social Correlates," in *Sexual Orientation: Toward Biological Understanding,* ed. L. Ellis and L. Ebertz (Westport, CT: Praeger Publishers, 1997).

18. Brian S. Mustanski and J. Michael Bailey, "A Therapist's Guide to the Genetics of Human Sexual Orientation," *Sexual and Relationship Therapy* 18 (2003): 1468–79.

19. R. Plomin, J. C. DeFries, G. E. McClearn, and M. Rutter, *Behavioral Genetics* (New York: Freeman, 1997).

20. J. M. Bailey and R. C. Pillard, "A Genetic Study of Male Sexual Orientation," *Archives of General Psychiatry* 48 (1991): 1089–96; Bailey and Pillard, "Genetics of Human Sexual Orientation," *Annual Review of Sex Research* 6 (1995): 126–50; J. M. Bailey, R. C. Pillard, M. C. Neale, and Y. Agyei, "Heritable Factors Influence Sexual Orientation in Women," *Archives of General Psychiatry* 50 (1993): 217–23.

21. J. M. Bailey, M. P. Dunne, and N. G. Martin, "Genetic and Environmental Influences on Sexual Orientation and Its Correlates in an Australian Twin Sample," *Journal of Personality and Social Psychology* 78 (2000): 524–36; K. S. Kendler, L. M. Thornton, S. E. Gilman, and R. C. Kessler, "Sexual Orientation in a U.S. National Sample of Twin and Nontwin Sibling Pairs," *American Journal of Psychiatry* 157 (2000): 1843–46.

22. S. D. Zhang and W. F. Odenwald, "Misexpression of the White (W) Gene Triggers Male-Male Courtship in Drosophila," *Proceedings of the National Academy of Sciences of the United States of America* 92 (1995): 5525–29.

23. Reported in Timothy F. Murphy, "Genetic Science and Discrimination," *Chronicle of Higher Education: Chronicle Review,* June 4, 2004, http://chronicle.com/.

24. Andrea Camperio-Ciani, Francesca Corna, and Laudio Capiluppi, "Evidence for Maternally Inherited Factors Favouring Male Homosexuality and Promoting Female Fecundity," *Proceedings of the Royal Society of London* B, 271 (2004): 2217–21.

25. Simon LeVay, "A Difference in Hypothalamic Structure Between Heterosexual and Homosexual Men," *Science* 253 (1991): 1034–37.

26. Quoted in D. Nimmons, "Sex and the Brain," *Discover,* March 1994, 64–71.

27. S. M. Breedlove, "Sex on the Brain," *Nature* 389 (1997): 801.

28. Simon LeVay, *The Sexual Brain* (Cambridge, MA: Bradford Books/MIT Press, 1993).

29. K. Larkin, J. A. Resko, F. Stormshak, J. N. Stellflug, and C. E. Roselli, "Neuroanatomical Correlates of Sex and Sexual Partner Preference in Sheep" (paper read at the Society for Neuroscience convention, Orlando, FL: November 2002); C. E. Roselli, J. A. Resko, and F. Stormshak, "Hormonal Influences on Sexual Partner Preference in Rams," *Archives of Sexual Behavior* 31 (2002): 43–49.

30. Rahman and Wilson, "Born Gay?"

31. Laura Allen and Roger Gorski, "Sexual Orientation and the Size of the Anterior Commissure in the Human Brain," *Proceedings of the National Academy of Sciences* 89 (1992): 7199–7202.

32. Brian Gladue, "The Biopsychology of Sexual Orientation," *Current Directions in Psychological Science* 3 (1994): 150–54.

33. Gunter Dorner, *Hormones and Brain Differentiation* (Amsterdam: Elsevier Scientific, 1976); G. Dorner, "Neuroendocrine Response to Estrogen and Brain Differentiation in Heterosexuals, Homosexuals, and Transsexuals," *Archives of Sexual Behavior* 17 (1988): 57–75.

34. J. Money, "Sin, Sickness, or Status? Homosexual Gender Identity and Psychoneuroendocrinology," *American Psychologist* 42 (1987): 384–99.

35. L. Ellis and M. A. Ames, "Neurohormonal Functioning and Sexual Orientation: A Theory of Homosexuality-Heterosexuality," *Psychological Bulletin* 101 (1987): 233–58; B. A. Gladue, "Hormones and Neuroendocrine Factors in Atypical Human Sexual Behavior," in *Pedophilia: Biosocial Dimensions,* ed. J. R. Feierman (New York: Springer-Verlag, 1990); H. F. L. Meyer-Bahlburg, "Psychoneuroendocrinology and Sexual Pleasure: The Aspect of Sexual Orientation," in *Sexual Nature/Sexual Culture,* ed. P. R. Abramson and S. D. Pinkerton (Chicago: Univ. of Chicago Press, 1995).

36. R. Blanchard, "Birth Order and Sibling Sex Ratio in Homosexual Versus Heterosexual Males and Females," *Annual Review of Sex Research,* 8 (1997): 27–67; Blanchard, "Fraternal Birth Order and the Maternal Immune Hypothesis of Male Homosexuality," *Hormones and Behavior,* 40 (2001): 105–14; Anthony F. Bogaert, "Number of Older Brothers and Sexual Orientation: New Tests and the Attraction/Behavior Distinction in Two National Probability Samples," *Journal of Personality and Social Psychology* 84 (2003): 644–52.

37. R. J. Rose, J. Kaprio, T. Winter, D. M. Dick, R. J. Viken, L. Pulkkinen, and M. Koskenvuo, "Femininity and Fertility in Sisters with Twin Brothers: Prenatal Androgenization? Cross-Sex Socialization?" *Psychological Science* 13 (2002): 263–66.

38. B. S. Mustanski, J. M. Bailey, and S. Kaspar, "Dermatoglyphics, Handedness, Sex, and Sexual Orientation," *Archives of Sexual Behavior* 31 (2002): 113–22; G. Sanders, M. Sjodin, and M. de Chastelaine, "On the Elusive Nature of Sex Differences in Cognition: Hormonal Influences Contributing to Within-Sex Variation," *Archives of Sexual Behavior* 31 (2002): 145–52.

39. Jeff Hall and Doreen Kimura, "Dermatoglyphic Assymetry and Sexual Orientation in Men," *Behavioral Neuroscience* 108 (1994): 1203–6.

40. M. L. Lalumière, R. Blanchard, and K. J. Zucker, "Sexual Orientation and Handedness in Men and Women: A Meta-Analysis," *Psychological Bulletin* 126 (2000): 575–92.

41. D. McFadden, "Masculinization Effects in the Auditory System," *Archives of Sexual Behavior* 31 (2002): 99–111.

42. Qazi Rahman, Glenn D. Wilson, and Sharon Abrahams, "Biosocial Factors, Sexual Orientation and Neurocognitive Functioning," *Psychoneuroendocrinology* 29 (2004): 867–81.

43. Q Rahman and K. Silber, "Sexual Orientation and the Sleep Waking Cycle," *Archives of Sexual Behavior* 29 (2000): 127–134.

44. Rahman and Wilson, "Born Gay?"

45. L. M. Diamond, "Sexual Identity, Attractions, and Behavior Among Young Sexual-Minority Women over a 2-Year Period," *Developmental Psychology* 36 (2000): 241–50; L. A. Peplau and L. D. Garnets, "A New Paradigm for Understanding Women's Sexuality and Sexual Orientation," *Journal of Social Issues* 56 (2000): 329–50.

46. Roy F. Baumeister, "Gender Differences in Erotic Plasticity: The Female Sex Drive As Socially Flexible and Responsive," *Psychological Bulletin* 126 (2000): 347–74.

47. Lisa M. Diamond, "What Does Sexual Orientation Orient? A Biobehavioral Model Distinguishing Romantic Love and Sexual Desire," *Psychological Review* 110 (2003): 173–92.

48. Bem, "Exotic Becomes Erotic: Developmental Theory"; Bem, "Is EBE Theory Supported by the Evidence? Is It Androcentric? A Reply to Peplau et al.," *Psychological Review* 105 (1998): 395–98; Bem, "Exotic Becomes Erotic: Biological Correlates."

49. Joseph LeDoux, *Synaptic Self: How Our Brains Become Who We Are* (New York: Viking, 2002), 5.

Chapter 6: Changing Sexual Orientation

1. Martin Seligman, *What You Can Change and What You Can't* (New York: Knopf, 1944).

2. Scott Bidstrup, "Gay Marriage: The Arguments and the Motives," n.d., http://www.bidstrup.com/marriage.htm.

3. "Religious Beliefs Underpin Opposition to Homosexuality: Republicans Unified, Democrats Split on Gay Marriage," November 18, 2003, http://people_press.org/reports/display.php3?ReportID=197. Among "high commitment" evangelicals, 73 percent thought sexual orientation could be changed, 17 percent thought not, with the rest not knowing. Among mainline Protestants, 26 percent thought it could be changed, 50 percent thought not. Among white Catholics, 30 percent thought it could be, 54 percent thought not.

4. Matt. 23:4 (TEV).

5. Elizabeth Moberly, *Homosexuality: A New Christian Ethic* (Cambridge: James Clarke, 1983); Joseph Nicolosi, *Reparative Therapy of Male Homosexuality: A New Clinical Approach* (Northvale, NJ: Jason Aronson, 1991).

6. Mike Haley, quoted in Glenn T. Stanton and Dr. Bill Maier, *Marriage on Trial: The Case Against Same-Sex Marriage and Parenting* (Downers Grove, IL: InterVarsity Press, 2004), 185.

7. Public Affairs Office, American Psychological Association, "Answers to Your

Questions About Sexual Orientation and Homosexuality," http://www.apa.org/pubinfo/answers.html.

8. American Academy of Pediatrics, "Homosexuality and Adolescence" (1993), quoted in American Psychological Association, "Just the Facts About Sexual Orientation and Youth," http://www.apa.org/pi/lgbc/publications/justthefacts.html.

9. National Association of Social Workers, "Lesbian, Gay, and Bisexual Issues" (approved by Delegate Assembly, August 1996), quoted in American Psychological Association, "Just the Facts."

10. American Psychiatric Association, "Position Statements on Therapies Focused on Attempts to Change Sexual Orientation ('Reparative' or 'Conversion' Therapies)" (adopted December 1998), in American Psychiatric Association, "Fact Sheet: Gay, Lesbian and Bisexual Issues" (2000), http://www.psych.org/public_info/gaylesbianbisealissues22701.pdf.

11. Tim LaHaye, *The Unhappy Gays* (Wheaton, IL: Tyndale Press, 1978).

12. Erwin Lutzer, *The Truth About Same-Sex Marriage* (Chicago: Moody Press, 2004), 37.

13. http://exodus.to/about_exodus_mission.shtml and http://exodus.to/about_exodus_healing.shtml.

14. Quoted in Candi Cushman, "Now That's a Family," *Citizen,* June 2004, http://www.family.org/cforum/citizenmag/coverstory/a0032241.cfm.

15. Jeff Ford, "Reparative Therapy: A Pseudo Science," http://jgford.homestead.com/index-ns4.html, quoted in Ralph Blair, *Record: Newsletter of Evangelicals Concerned,* summer 1990, 1.

16. Quoted in *Record: Newsletter of Evangelicals Concerned* spring 2002, 1.

17. http://www.courage.org.uk/index.shtml.

18. Clint Trout's autobiographical story appeared in *Finally Free* (Washington, DC: Human Rights Campaign Foundation, July 2000).

19. Bob Davies, Exodus press release (September 11, 2000), http://www.exodusnorthamerica.org/news/pressrel/a0000534.html.

20. Ralph Blair, personal correspondence, August 2, 2000.

21. Bob Davies, Exodus statement (October 3, 2000), http://www.exodusnorthamerica.org/news/pressrel/a0000538.html.

22. "Former 'Ex-Gay' Speaks Out in Gay Press," Exodus International press release, September 11, 2000, exodus.to/news_2000_0911.shtml.

23. Bob Davies, Exodus statement (August 11, 2000), exodus.to/news_0811.shtml.

24. ChristianLesbians.com, "What About the Ex-Gay Movement?" http://www.christianlesbians.com/articles/lesbianliving.php?id=000007 (accessed August 18, 2004).

25. *American Family Association Journal,* May 2000.

26. *Christianity Today,* January 7, 2002.

27. Robert Spitzer, "200 Subjects Who Claim to Have Changed Their Sexual Orientation from Homosexual to Heterosexual" (paper presented at the American Psychiatric Association annual convention, New Orleans, May 9, 2001). This paper was later published as "Can Some Gay Men and Lesbians Change Their Sexual Orientation? 200 Participants Reporting a Change from Homosexual to Heterosexual Orientation," *Archives of Sexual Behavior,* 32 (2003): 403–17.

28. NARTH: The National Association for Research and Therapy of Homosexuality.

29. Mike Yaconelli, "Fantasy Christianity," *Wittenburg Door* no. 94 (December 1986–January 1987).

30. William Masters and Virginia E. Johnson, *Homosexuality in Perspective* (New York: Lippincott Williams and Wilkens, 1979).

31. Donald Wildmon, "National 'Coming out of Homosexuality Day' Helps Homosexuals Leave Lifestyle," n.d., included in the National Coming Out of Homosexuality Day press packet (October 1997).

32. The Johnston exposé was reported in the gay press (e.g., Laura Douglas-Brown, "Ex-Gay Leader Experiences 'Moral Fall': Johnston Allegedly Had Sex with Men Without Disclosing He Is HIV-Positive," *SouthernVoice.com,* August 8, 2003) and acknowledged by his conservative friends (e.g., Peter LaBarbera, "When a Friend Falls," Concerned Women for America, n.d., http://www.cwfa.org/articles/4411/CFI/cfreport/index.htm.

Chapter 7: What the Bible Does and Doesn't Say

1. John Boswell, *Christianity, Social Tolerance, and Homosexuality* (Chicago: Univ. of Chicago Press, 1980), 42.

2. Don Blosser, "Why Does the Bible Divide Us? A Conversation with Scripture on Same-Gender Attraction," in *To Continue the Dialogue: Biblical Interpretation and Homosexuality,* ed. C. Norman Kraus (Telford, PA: Pandora Press, 2001), 121–47. Blosser draws upon G. Johannes Botterweck, "Yada," in *The Theological Dictionary of the Old Testament* (Grand Rapids, MI: Wm. B. Eerdmans Publishing Company, 1975), where Botterweck identified ten ways in which the Hebrew word *yadah,* "to know," has been used in English translations of the Bible. The nonsexual interpretation of the incident in Genesis 19 was also described in detail in Derrick Sherwin Bailey, *Homosexuality and the Western Christian Tradition* (London: Longmans, Green, 1955).

3. The National Center for Victims of Crime, "Male Rape," http://www.ncvc.org/.

4. Seymour M. Hersch, "Torture at Abu Ghraib," *New Yorker,* May 10, 2004.

5. "N.Y. Officer Jailed over Assault Case," follow-up story, BBC News, Sept. 22, 2002, http://news.bbc.co.uk/2/hi/americas/2274379.stm.

6. Jere Longman, "Year After Assaults, Play Begins but Pain Never Ends," *New York Times,* September 29, 2004.

7. http://www.spr.org/.

8. Stephen Donaldson, "The Rape Crisis Behind Bars," *New York Times,* December 29, 1993, http://www.spr.org/en/sprnews/pre2002/doc_01_nyt.html.

9. *The Jewish Study Bible* (Oxford and New York: Oxford Univ. Press, 2004), 251.

10. For examples, see Prov. 6:16–19, 11:1, 12:22, 16:5, and 20:23.

11. See Tim LaHaye and Beverly LaHaye, *The Act of Marriage* (Grand Rapids, MI: Zondervan, 1976), 275. For a complete discussion of conservative Christian authors who have argued for sexual relations during a wife's menstruation, see Letha Dawson Scanzoni and Virginia Ramey Mollenkott, *Is the Homosexual My Neighbor?* 2d ed. (San Francisco: HarperSanFrancisco, 1994), chap. 8.

12. During a roundtable discussion of "A New Sexual Ethics for Judaism?" in the September–October 1993 issue of *Tikkun,* it was pointed out that some Talmudic rabbis were persuaded that the particular type of rebelliousness described in the Deuteronomy passage doesn't exist among children and is therefore not applicable to today. The panel members were then asked to ponder whether such a reading could be similarly applied to questions about homosexuality as it is known today.

13. *Jewish Study Bible*, sidebar notes for 1 Kings 14:24.

14. L. William Countryman, *Dirt, Greed, and Sex: Sexual Ethics in the New Testament and Their Implications for Today* (Philadelphia: Fortress Press, 1988), 37–38. For some of the debates among scholars about the existence of male cult prostitution, see *Jewish Study Bible,* commentary on Deut. 23: 18–19 and on 1 Kings 14:24, which lists other possible nonsexual idolatrous practices that the original Hebrew word might refer to. See also Phyllis A. Bird, "The Bible in Christian Ethical Deliberation," in *Homosexuality, Science, and the "Plain Sense" of Scripture,* ed. David L. Balch (Grand Rapids, MI: Eerdmans, 2000), 170–73.

15. Robin Scroggs, *The New Testament and Homosexuality* (Philadelphia: Fortress Press, 1983), 86. See also William R. Schoedel, "Same-Sex Eros: Paul and the Greco-Roman Tradition," in *Homosexuality, Science, and the "Plain Sense" of Scripture,* ed. David L. Balch (Grand Rapids, MI: Eerdmans, 2000), 63–30; and Allen Verhey, *Remembering Jesus: Christian Community, Scripture, and the Moral Life* (Grand Rapids, MI: Eerdmans, 2002), 232.

16. Scroggs, *New Testament.* See esp. his summary in chaps. 7 and 8.

17. The New English Translation Bible was originally developed for the Internet. See http://www.Bible.org/page.asp?page_id=10.

18. Boswell, *Christianity,* 158, 203–5.

19. Countryman, *Dirt, Greed, and Sex,* 112; Robert Jewett, "The Social Context and Implications of Homoerotic References in Romans," in *Homosexuality, Science, and the "Plain Sense" of Scripture,* ed. David L. Balch (Grand Rapids, MI: Eerdmans,

2000), 223—41. See also Scroggs, *New Testament and Homosexuality*, for a summary of other scholars pointing out the context and purpose of Paul's argument.

20. Reta Halteman Finger, "What Can We Do When We Don't Agree? Christian Tolerance in Romans 14:1–15:6," in *To Continue the Dialogue: Biblical Interpretation and Homosexuality*, ed. C. Norman Kraus (Telford, PA: Pandora Press).

21. Verhey, *Remembering Jesus*, 237.

22. See Wisd. of Sol., chaps. 13 and 14.

23. Finger, "What Can We Do," 213.

24. Blosser, "Why Does the Bible Divide Us?" 143.

Chapter 8: What God Has Joined Together?

1. Richard Rodriguez, "Essay: American Family," *NewsHour*, March 8, 2004, http://www.pbs.org/newshour/essays-dialogues.html.

2. Bob Egelko, "Top State Court Voids S.F.'s Gay Marriages: A Mayor Overruled," *San Francisco Chronicle*, August 13, 2004.

3. Robert A. J. Gagnon, "Why 'Gay Marriage' Is Wrong," http://www.robgagnon.net/homoPresbyTodayArticle.htm. This is a longer version of an article that appeared in the September 2004 issue of *Presbyterians Today*.

4. Richard Mouw, as quoted in Rob Mall, "Civil Unions: Would a Marriage by Any Other Name Be the Same?" *Christianity Today*, March 8, 2004, http://www.christianitytoday.com/ct/2004/110/11.0.html.

5. George Lakoff and Mark Johnson, *Metaphors We Live By* (Chicago: Univ. of Chicago Press, 1980), 5.

6. Bernadette J. Brooten, *Love Between Women: Early Christian Responses to Female Homoeroticism* (Chicago: Univ. of Chicago Press, 1996), 359.

7. Brooten, *Love Between Women*, 361.

8. Rosemary R. Ruether, "The Personalization of Sex," in *From Machismo to Mutuality*, by Rosemary R. Ruether and Eugene C. Bianchi (New York: Paulist Press, 1976), as reprinted in *Homosexuality and Ethics*, ed. Edward Batchelor Jr. (New York: Pilgrim Press, 1980), 29.

9. Letha Dawson Scanzoni and Nancy A. Hardesty, *All We're Meant to Be: Biblical Feminism for Today* (Grand Rapids, MI: Eerdmans, 1994 revised edition; originally published 1974); Virginia Ramey Mollenkott, *Women, Men, and the Bible* (New York: Crossroad, 1988 revised edition; originally published 1977).

10. See Willard M. Swartley, *Slavery, Sabbath, War, and Women: Case Issues in Biblical Interpretation* (Scottdale, PA: Herald Press, 1983).

11. Margaret Nutting Ralph, *And God Said What? An Introduction to Biblical Literary Forms*, rev. ed. (New York: Paulist Press, 2003), 275.

12. James Dobson, *Marriage Under Fire: Why We Must Win This Battle* (Sisters, OR: Multnomah Publishers, 2004), 11–12.

13. Dobson, *Marriage Under Fire*, 12.

Chapter 9: Gay Marriage

1. The quote from Rick Santorum is taken from remarks he made on July 14, 2004, to the U.S. Senate before a vote related to the Federal Marriage Amendment. The quote from Maggie Gallagher is taken from "The Stakes: Why We Need Marriage," *National Review*, July 14, 2003, http://www.national-review.com/. James Dobson's quote is taken from an address he made to the National Press Club on June 25, 2004; it was rebroadcast on C-Span. Charles Colson's quote is taken from a letter he wrote in December 2003 that was addressed to "All BreakPoint Supporters."

2. Colson, letter to "All BreakPoint Supporters."

3. George W. Bush, campaign rally (Wisconsin, July 14, 2004); quoted on www.abcnews.go.com and elswhere.

4. Harold Jaffe, "Whatever Happened to the U.S. AIDS Epidemic?" *Science* 305 (2004): 1243 44.

5. Susan D. Cochran, "Emerging Issues in Research on Lesbians' and Gay Men's Mental Health: Does Sexual Orientation Really Matter?" *American Psychologist* 56 (2001): 932–47; Gary Remafedi, Simone French, Mary Story, Michael D. Resnick, and Robert Blum, "The Relationship Between Suicide Risk and Sexual Orientation: Results of a Population-Based Study," *American Journal of Public Health* 88:1 (1998): 57–60.

6. Centers for Disease Control, "Cases by Exposure Category."

7. Jaffe, "Whatever Happened," 1243–44.

8. William N. Eskridge Jr., "The Emerging Menu of Quasi-Marriage Options," *FindLaw's Writ: Legal Commentary*, http://writ.news.findlaw.com/commentary/20000707_eskridge.html.

9. Jonathan Rauch, *Gay Marriage: Why It Is Good for Gays, Good for Straights, and Good for America* (New York: Times Books, 2004), 71.

10. Gottman Institute, "12-Year Study of Gay and Lesbian Couples," http://www.gottman.com/research/projects/gaylesbian.

11. Esther Rothblum, personal correspondence, July 4, 2004.

12. Lawrence A. Kurdek, "Are Gay and Lesbian Cohabiting Couples *Really* Different from Heterosexual Married Couples?" *Journal of Marriage and Family*, 66 (2004): 880-900; Sondra E. Solomon, Esther D. Rothblum, and Kimberly F. Balsam, "Pioneers in Partnership: Lesbian and Gay Male Couples in Civil Unions Compared with Those Not in Civil Unions, and Married Heterosexual Siblings," *Journal of Family Psychology* 18 (2004): 275–286.

13. Linda Waite and Maggie Gallagher, *The Case for Marriage: Why Married People Are Happier, Healthier, and Better Off Financially* (New York: Broadway Books, 2000), 17.

14. General Accounting Office, "Defense of Marriage Act: Update to Prior Report," Report Number GAO–04–353R, released February 24, 2004, http://www.gao.gov/atext/d04353r.txt.

15. King David's wives and/or the mothers of his children include Michael (1 Sam. 18:27), Abigail (1 Sam. 25:39), Ahinoam of Jezreel (1 Sam. 25:43), Eglah (2 Sam. 3:4–5), Maacah (2 Sam. 3:3), Abital (2 Sam. 3:4–5), Haggith (2 Sam. 3:4–5), and Bathsheba (2 Sam. 12:24). He also had ten concubines (2 Sam. 15:16).

16. Hendrik Hartog, "What Gay Marriage Teaches about the History of Marriage," lecture presented at the Organization of American Historians, March 28, 2004, http://hnn.us/articles/4400.html.

17. Charles Colson, letter to "BreakPoint colleague," September 22, 2003.

18. *Family Research Council* "In Focus" essay by Peter Sprigg, "Questions and answers: What's wrong with letting same-sex couples marry?," Undated issue No. 256, http://www.frc.org/get.cfm?i=IF03H01.

19. Robert Benne and Gerald McDermott, "Speaking Out: Why Gay Marriage Would Be Harmful," *Christianity Today*, February 16, 2004, http://www.christianitytoday.com/ct/2004/107/41.0.html.

20. "The New Stay-at-Home Parent: Ward and Ward Cleaver," *BreakPoint WorldView Magazine*, May 2004, 31.

21. Census Bureau data reported in Ginia Bellafante, "Two Fathers, with One Happy to Stay at Home," *New York Times*, January 12, 2004, http://www.nytimes.com/.

22. American Psychological Association, "Resolution on Sexual Orientation and Marriage: Research Summary" (resolution adopted by the Council of Representatives, 2004). See also Susan Golombok, Beth Perry, Amanda Burston, Clare Murray, Julie Mooney-Somers, Madeline Stevens, and Jean Golding, "Children with Lesbian Parents: A Community Study," *Developmental Psychology* 39 (2003): 20–33.

23. Charlotte J. Patterson, "Lesbian and Gay Parents and Their Children: Summary of Research Findings" (paper prepared for the American Psychological Association, May 2004, to appear at http://www.apa.org/). Whether couples are same-sex or opposite-sex, about one in four couples with a child include a stay-at-home parent (according to Cenus Bureau data reported in Bellafante, "Two Fathers").

24. Alice Bengel, "Same-Sex Couples' Children Are Doing Fine," *Virginian-Pilot*, August 5, 2004. This article originally appeared in the *Atlanta Journal-Constitution*.

25. Amy Smith, "Fostering Family Values," *Austin Chronicle*, May 2, 2003.

26. Family Research Council, "Culture Facts" (mailing, April 9, 2004).

27. David P. Schmitt, "Universal Sex Differences in the Desire for Sexual Variety: Tests from 52 Nations, 6 Continents, and 13 Islands," *Journal of Personality and Social Psychology* 85 (2003): 85–104. For our purposes, Professor Schmitt kindly separated out data for those not currently married or in relationships (personal correspondence, July 16, 2004).

28. Roger Doyle, "Gay and Lesbian Census," *Scientific American*, March, 2005, 28;

Suzanne Herel, Rona Marech, Ilene Lelchuk, "Numbers put face on a phenomenon: Most who married are middle-aged, have college degrees," *San Francisco Chronicle,* March 18, 2004, A-1, and http://sfgate.com.

29. For citations of major studies, see David G. Myers, *Psychology,* 7th ed. (New York: Worth Publishers, 2004).

30. Steven Pinker, *How the Mind Works* (New York: Norton, 1997), 474.

31. Charles Krauthammer, "When John and Jim Say, 'I Do,'" *Time,* July 22, 1996.

32. Antonin Scalia, dissenting opinion on Lawrence v. Texas (02-102), http://supct.law.cornell.edu/supct/html/02-102.ZD.html.

33. Focus on the Family, "Is Marriage in Jeopardy?" Booklet AP031A.

34. Amitai Etzioni, *The Spirit of Community: Rights, Responsibilities, and the Communitarian Agenda* (New York: Crown, 1993), 177.

35. Jonathan Rauch, "The Way We Live Now: Power of Two," *New York Times,* March 7, 2004, 125, www.nytimes.com/.

36. Rauch, "The Way We Live Now."

37. David Brooks, "The Power of Marriage," *New York Times,* November 22, 2003.

38. *Los Angeles Times,* April 10, 2004, as reported by Associated Press.

39. Robert Gagnon, "Gays and the Bible: A Response to Walter Wink," *Christian Century,* August 14–27, 2003.

40. Sara L. Boesser, *Silent Lives: How High a Price* (Lanham, MD: Hamilton Books, Univ. Press of America, 2004), 70.

41. Ralph Blair, *Review,* fall 2003 (http://www.ecinc.org/Reviews/rvfall_2003.htm).

42. Rauch, *Gay Marriage,* 92.

43. Bob McGrew, "Why Conservatives Should Support Gay Marriage," *Stanford Review* 31:5 (2003), http://www.stanfordreview.org/.

44. Kimberly Blanton, "Unmarried Gay Couples Lose Health Benefits," *Boston Globe,* December 8, 2004.

45. Charles Colson, "Urgent Memo to All Breakpoint/Prison Fellowship Supporters," February 26, 2004. The article by Stanley Kurtz to which Colson refers is "The End of Marriage in Scandinavia: The 'Conservative Case' for Same-Sex Marriage Collapses," *Weekly Standard* 9:20 (2004), http://www.weeklystandard.com/.

46. M. V. Lee Badgett, "Prenuptial Jitters: Did Gay Marriage Destroy Heterosexual Marriage in Scandinavia?" *Slate,* May 20, 2004, http://slate.msn.com/.

47. Jonathan Haidt: with Craig Joseph: "Intuituve Ethics: How Innately Prepared Intuitions Generate Culturally Variable Virtues," *Daedalus* (2004, Spring), 55–66; with Matthew A. Hersh, "Sexual Morality: The Cultures and Emotions of Conservatives and Liberals," *Journal of Applied Social Psychology* 31 (2001): 199–221.

48. Rauch, *Gay Marriage,* 191.

49. Sean Captain, "My Turn: Proud Bachelor Turned Marrying Man—Sort of," *Newsweek,* March 8, 2004.

Epilogue

1. American Psychological Association and New Jersey Psychological Association, "Amici Curiae Brief in Support of Plaintiffs-Appellants," October 25, 2004, index summary and pp. 32–34 (www.lambdalegal.org/binary-data/ LAMBDA_PDF/pdf/320.pdf, page: 185).

2. Quoted in Martin E. Marty, "The Desecration of Civic Discourse," *Los Angeles Times,* October 18, 1998.

3. Macky Alston, "My Blessed Gay Marriage," http://www.beliefnet.com/story/ 129/story_12937_1.html.

4. Mark G. Toulouse, "Muddling Through: The Church and Sexuality/Homosexuality," in *Homosexuality, Science, and the "Plain Sense" of Scripture,* ed. David L. Balch (Grand Rapids, MI: Eerdmans, 2000), 42.

5. Toulouse, "Muddling Through," 11.

6. Toulouse, "Muddling Through," 34.

7. Toulouse, "Muddling Through," 34.

Appendix A: Why Marriage Matters

1. Norval Glenn, Steven Nock, and Linda Waite, "Why Marriage Matters: Twenty-One Conclusions from the Social Sciences," *American Experiment Quarterly* 5 (2002): 34–44.

Appendix B: Attitudes Are Changing

1. Mel White, "Why We Can't Wait. . . to End This Debate," www.soulforce. org/main/wecantwait.shtml.

2. Adam Goodheart, "Small-Town Gay America," *The New York Times,* Sunday, November 23, 2003.

Index

Plus:

Plus: **Insights, Interviews, and More**

The authors of *What God Has Joined Together* interview each other

Letha: How have your ideas about sexual orientation and same-sex marriage developed?

Dave: I began my adult life presuming that sexual orientation is a moral choice, and that the Bible resoundingly condemns homosexuality. I therefore empathize with, and am not offended by, others who presume the same. My journey from there to what I now believe—that sexual orientation is a natural, enduring disposition and that the Bible doesn't have a word to say about "sexual orientation" or "homosexuality" (and very little to say about same-sex behaviors in specific contexts)—began when Ralph Blair, founder of Evangelicals Concerned (a gay support organization), visited my campus and I began reading his occasional newsletter. It continued through friendships and conversations with gay and gay-supporting students and colleagues, and through reading various books and articles. These included materials from across the spectrum, including your and Virginia Mollenkott's pioneering book, *Is the Homosexual My Neighbor?*

For me a very big influence has also been reading psychological and biological science research on sexual orientation, and reporting on such in my introductory psychology texts. I feel like the scientists who didn't expect to believe in global warming or in the ancient history of the earth and its species but have been persuaded by the accumulating evidence to change their minds.

Reading the research literature was also persuading me of the benefits of marriage and the human need to belong. And that led me to stand up for monogamy. On balance, I do believe, the world would be a happier and healthier place if, for all people, love, sex, and marriage went together. (Take out the words "for all people" and this sounds pretty conservative, and it remains moderately conservative, methinks, even with those three words included.)

Letha: So what led you to speak out, and to propose this book?

Dave: I'm motivated to write, and to offer information to the public sphere, whenever I'm struck by the thought that "Hey, people ought to know about this!"That is what has led me to write about the characteristics of happy lives, about the powers and perils of intuition, about my experiences with hearing loss and some effective ways to deal with it, and now about the benefits of marriage and the realities of sexual orientation. Seeing the culture at war over gay marriage and seeing Christendom at war over the ordination of gay people to church office I wondered if we might help bridge the divide.

Most of what I have to offer in my speaking and writing is information—about the benefits of marriage (which folks on the left might want to consider incorporating into their thinking) and information about sexual orientation and the longing for belonging (which folks on the right might want to consider incorporating into their thinking). I don't expect everyone to arrive at our conclusions. I simply want to offer information that people, whatever their views, might want to be aware of and that might inform their own understanding.

Dave: So, tell me, how did *you*, in the much less accepting climate of the 1970s, come to engage this topic and to co-author *Is the Homosexual My Neighbor*?

Letha: I don't think I chose this topic so much as the topic chose me, a very unlikely spokesperson. I started out with the same assumptions about homosexuality as you, Dave. I had given little thought to the topic when I first began writing about love, marriage, gender issues, and sexuality in the 1960s and 1970s. Up until that time, I had heard only that A) homosexuality was a moral choice and B) it was a *bad* moral choice. Not only was it considered sinful, it was also considered a sickness and a crime. Because of these religious and societal attitudes, a sense of fear surrounded the topic, and Christians tended to experience a sense of shame and revulsion at the thought of even talking about it.

Around that time, psychologist George Weinberg coined the term *homophobia,* and I realized the term summed up precisely what I was observing among many Christians—an intense anxiety about homosexuality that resulted in suspicion of any close same-sex friendship. So, in 1974 I wrote an article for *Christianity Today* titled "On Friendship and Homosexuality" in which I talked about how, despite the Scriptural teaching that the world should know we are Christians by our love for each other, homophobia was making many Christians afraid of feelings of love. Some Christians were suspicious of any verbal expressions of affection between persons of the same sex and even of hugs. Yet we lived in a world starved for touch. At the time I wrote that article, I said that although I disagreed with an emerging gay theology movement, I thought the movement was doing other Christians a favor by pointing out biblical examples that showed that "persons of the same sex can, did, and do love each other." My emphasis was on *emotional* connection that did not necessarily mean— or lead to—sexual expression. In writing my article, I had been thinking of one-soul relationships, not one-flesh relationships.

But like you, I was doing research in social science literature for my writing and was coming to new understandings about sexual orientation. I had also been re-examining traditional assumptions about what the Bible says about male and female roles, and I had written about gender equality and social justice for women. And I was writing a book on sex education in the Christian home. For these reasons, I couldn't ignore questions about homosexuality. I especially had to address the topic while co-authoring a college textbook, *Men, Women, and Change: A Sociology of Marriage and Family*, with my then-husband John Scanzoni. In it, we had a section titled

"Gay Marriage."That was in 1976—three decades ago! So I've had a long time to think about it.

Dave: So how did your emerging thinking about gay marriage intersect with your evangelical faith?

Letha: Three other happenings in the early 1970s caused me to reconsider my assumptions about homosexuality in relation to my faith. Until then, I had been compartmentalizing the two, objectively writing about homosexual relationships from a social science viewpoint but yet not able to reconcile my scientific knowledge with my understanding of Scripture.

First, I began corresponding with a woman who had been a guest speaker for a college discussion group that I helped lead in my church in the late 1960s. At the time she spoke to us, she was engaged in a ministry to help gay men and lesbians move away from homosexuality. But when I wrote to ask her some questions about it several years later, she had completely changed her mind, having become aware of some of the latest biblical scholarship taking place and having met gay Christians whom she described as displaying the gifts of the Spirit. Because so many people thought of homosexual persons only in terms of promiscuity, she said she was persuaded that the answer wasn't in trying to change them into heterosexuals, which was impossible, but rather to let them marry the person they loved even though they were of the same sex. That was one of the first times I heard about the concept of same-sex marriage. For a time, this woman and I wrote back and forth, and I at first argued with her from both a natural law perspective and from selected scriptures. When I began restating her arguments and asking if I had correctly grasped what she meant (particularly on faithful, covenantal unions between two persons of the same sex), I found myself undergoing a paradigm shift.

The second happening during this time was my meeting Virginia Ramey Mollenkott when we were both asked to speak at an evangelical seminary. We found we had been

185

Plus: **Insights, Interviews, and More**

reading and appreciating each other's writings, so we began a correspondence. At some point we decided to collaborate on a book on Christian ethics in which we would discuss various issues in our rapidly changing society that Christians were struggling with. We planned chapters on abortion, homosexuality, divorce, free speech, censorship, and other topics. We had decided that I would write the chapter on homosexuality (because of all the research I had been doing for my other books), and Virginia would write the chapters on censorship and divorce. It was during our writing of this ethics book that Virginia revealed to me that she herself was a lesbian Christian, though closeted at the time. For me, this brought the subject "up close and personal," and we corresponded at length about our mutual struggles over this revelation. We never finished the planned ethics book, but instead worked together to enlarge the chapter on homosexuality and develop it into an entire book, which became *Is the Homosexual My Neighbor?* During this time, I thought a lot about chapter 10 of Acts, which tells the story of Peter, a devout, observant Jew who had understood that Gentiles were to be shunned as unclean and unwelcome in God's family but had his understanding completely turned around by a vision from God and a visit by a devout Gentile soldier. Peter at first argued with God, reminding God of the laws God had instituted in the scriptures; but in the end, he realized God accepted the Gentiles and so should he. I told Virginia she was my "Peter vision."

The third thing that happened during the 1970s was a huge controversy that erupted over a city ordinance adopted in Bloomington, Indiana, where I then lived. The law prohibited discrimination against gay people in housing, employment, education, and access to public accommodations. Conservative Christians saw it as a sign of moral decay, and their church leaders started a campaign to urge citizens "to prayerfully make it a matter of immediate personal decision: to shun the sodomites and their supporters, to use every lawful device to eliminate homosexual activity in this area, and to rededicate our community to standards set forth by God." Thousands of Christians signed that statement and took out a full-page newspaper ad with as many of the signatures as could be fitted on the page. I decided to interview people on all sides, including conservative ministers who feared the gay men and lesbians, gay people who feared the ministers, liberal pastors who saw justice and compassion toward gay people as being an expression of God's commandment to love as God loves us, and the director of the Kinsey Institute, who approached it from a social science researcher viewpoint. During my writing of this article ("Conservative Christians and Gay Civil Rights," *Christian Century*, Oct. 13, 1976), I saw that the homosexual question was at least three-sided, having a civil rights factor, a human factor, and a theological factor.

Dave: What response did you get when *Is the Homosexual My Neighbor?* was published in 1978?

Letha: Responses varied. I'm sure some people were upset and disappointed at the stand Virginia and I had taken, since we were well-known for our writings in evangelical circles. Some reactions and reviews were quite negative. And I was "disinvited" from one major speaking engagement because of it. But many other Christians were surprisingly positive. Even though they might not agree with our conclusions, many commended us for a scholarly and compassionate approach based on both Scripture and social science. And various churches used the book for discussion groups. What was especially gratifying, however, was the reception the book received from homosexual Christians and their loved ones. Many gay people said they felt it was a book they could give to their parents to read. And on almost every occasion where Virginia and I have spoken in all the years since the book's publication, one or more gay people have come up to us after a speech and said words such as these: "Your book saved my life. It made me see God loves me just as I am." Many have gone on to tell in detail how they had made plans to commit suicide, and just then ran across the book in a bookstore or library or were given a copy by someone. Hearing such stories about saved lives is probably the greatest reward any author could receive.

Letha: How about you, Dave? How has *your* writing on this topic impacted your life? Has your affiliation with a Christian college been affected by your coauthoring this book?

Dave: In interviews and conversation I think I've been asked that question more than any other. My affiliation is unaffected by this book, as I knew would be the case. My college respects the academic free marketplace. Here, as in nearly every other college, faculty are invited to discern and give witness to the truth as best they can. We contribute our information and conclusions, and welcome other people doing the same. Indeed, though I have confidence in the information and conclusions that you and I present, I have much more confidence in the free marketplace of ideas. My conviction is that, over time, wisdom and understanding will grow by a free exchange.

I hasten to add that individual faculty members do not speak for their colleges. Also, donors had best decide their support based not on whether they like or dislike what an individual faculty member is saying—that's a mere historical blip—but on whether they affirm the institution's mission, and whether they affirm the basic idea of a college as a wisdom-spawning free marketplace of ideas.

Letha: What has been the college's response?

Dave: In response to front page stories on our book in several Michigan newspapers, including the *Detroit Free Press,* my college reminded people, as have I, that I do not speak for it. It also stated that the college supports the academic freedom that enables its faculty to write from diverse perspectives.

Letha: What has been the response of others—particularly in your home area?

Dave: In the first five months after publication I received some 200 letters and e-mails, not counting a stream of newspaper letters to the editor, pro and con. I've heard from former students, some of whom I never realized were gay. I've heard from friends, from friends of the college, and from total strangers from around the country. Most have been kind and supportive, and seem to appreciate the effort to bridge the divide with a message that respects both marriage and the aspirations of gay and lesbian people.

About three dozen people, including some friends, have written to express their disappointment, dismay, or outrage. My understanding is that my college has heard from more such people. And we know that many more are quietly disapproving but too kind to say anything.

The critical communications that I've received have two things in common. First, they have been fair and appropriate. The letter writers express their convictions and then explain the reasons for them, often quoting Scripture. I respect these people, and have thanked them for writing.

Second, all but one of the critics seem not to have read our book or anything that either of us have written related to it. Rather, they are responding to a newspaper synopsis or to our provocative subtitle. I'd like to think that if they read the book they might find it more marriage- and Scripture-affirming than what they are imagining.

Letha: And what has been the response of people in your denomination?

Dave: I've heard, privately, from a number of appreciative pastors, and from some upset pastors. Also, I have testified at a nationally publicized trial of the president of one of my denomination's two seminaries. The trial was in response to his officiating at the Massachusetts marriage of his daughter and the woman she loves. It was an emotionally intense

Plus · **Insights, Interviews, and More**

experience for many of the three hundred or so people present. (As expected, he was suspended from his ministerial office.)

Although I can't say that I felt much grace and love that day, the attending delegates did listen respectfully. Moreover, they tabled overtures to establish new anti-gay denominational policies and instead wisely agreed to enter a three-year process of dialogue.

Dave: What do you think is at the root of these intense reactions that many people have to questions about sexual orientation? Why, given that same-sex marriage isn't one of the Bible's big issues, has this become for the culture and the church such a hot button issue?

Letha: I think much of it comes out of fear—fear of change in the well-ordered moral universe many people have simply taken for granted. This change is symbolic of so many other changes in perceptions of the world resulting from new understandings opened up by the physical and social sciences. People were once sure that the sun revolved around the earth, and to think otherwise was considered heresy and a contradiction of God's revelation in the Bible. That actually wasn't one of the Bible's "big issues" either, but it was certainly a "hot button" issue in the time and religious culture in which Galileo lived!

No doubt there is also some sense of revulsion, which, as we mention briefly in the book, causes people to justify their feelings by looking for biblical, moral, and "natural law" arguments to bolster their feelings.

Dave: So tell me, Letha, how do you respond to people who sharply disagree with your reading of Scripture? What do you say during an interview or after one of your talks when you've got no more than a minute or two to respond to someone who says (as people have said to me) "The Bible plainly says that men having sex with men is a sin"?

Letha: I first try to determine whether this is a sincere inquiry or an attempt to score points in an argument. Does the questioner honestly want to know how I understand such a passage? Or is this someone whose mind is already made up and who uses the question as a trap in a "gotcha" sort of way, just as the Pharisees of Jesus's day tried to trick him, hoping to accuse him of contradicting God's laws? If a one-minute reply really *is* expected, I might point out that we live in a bumper-sticker age where people expect quick simple sound bites, and some issues are too complex to answer in such a simplistic way.

I may talk about the gay person who told me about Christians who were quoting a similar verse in Leviticus that said men engaging in same-sex behavior should be put to death. He asked, "Does that mean Christians want to kill us?" The Bible "plainly" makes that "death penalty" statement, too (Lev. 20:13), but no one except a very disturbed person is going to say Scripture teaches we should kill homosexual people—or people who commit adultery, as is also stated in that same passage.

Most often, I talk briefly about biblical interpretation and how in *any* Bible reading we must seek first to understand how a message was understood by the original listeners to whom it was read. What is the cultural and historical context? We cannot know God's will by simply isolating verses. Jesus said a great deal about divorce and remarriage as being against God's ideal, and for the most part, those who speak out against same-sex relations have no trouble ignoring or reinterpreting those divorce passages, perhaps because they hit too close to home.

I also talk about the Bible's silence about same-sex covenantal love relationships and about sexual orientation as we know it today. And I would say it is thus better to apply basic biblical *principles* such as loving our neighbor as ourselves, not judging, and obeying Micah 6:8, where we are instructed to do justice, love compassion, and walk with God in

191

humility. This to me provides more guidance for approaching the issue of homosexual relationships than does pulling a single verse out of its context. I am reminded of a statement the Reverend William Sloan Coffin wrote to the National Conference of Catholic Bishops several years ago. He said, "For Christians, the problem is not how to reconcile homosexuality with scriptural passages that condemn it, but how to reconcile the rejection and punishment of homosexuals with the love of Christ."

Letha: As a psychologist, you keep up with social science literature. How would you answer those who say that by removing the mental illness label once applied to homosexuality, the American Psychological Association, the American Psychiatric Association, and other professional associations have yielded to what some people call a "homosexual agenda"?

Dave: It's true that "mental illness" is not so objectively defined as is, say, cancer. Is the boy rambunctious or does he have ADHD? In general, behavior gets labeled as a psychiatric disorder if it is deviant, distressful, and dysfunctional. Left-handedness is, in a statistical sense, deviant, but is not distressful or dysfunctional. Homosexuality can be distressful, as well as relatively infrequent, but much of the distress, including risk of suicide, stems from heterosexuals' attitudes and behavior. Promiscuity (among both straight and gay folks) puts people at risk of sexually transmitted diseases, but that leads us toward a case for monogamy, *not* a definition of homosexuality as an intrinsic mental illness among those who are comfortable with who they are and whom they love. Thus I think the American Psychiatric Association had good reason for declassifying homosexuality as a mental illness.

Letha: In the months since this book's first edition was published, has there been any new research on sexual orientation?

Dave: Yes, there has, and the new data continue to strengthen the growing recognition among scientists (and among more and more evangelical Christians as well) that sexual orientation is a natural disposition (and most clearly so for males). For example, when exposed to male sex-related odors, gay men's brains react similarly to straight women's. Another recent experiment confirms that with the manipulation of a single gene, fruit flies display same-sex attraction. These new discoveries add to a dozen other you-never-would-have-guessed revelations of gay-straight differences in things ranging from brain centers to fingerprint patterns to skill at mentally rotating geometric figures.

And there's more to come. One major study on the horizon is a five-year, $2.5 million National Institutes of Health-funded study of DNA from a thousand families with two or more gay brothers, in search of genes that influence sexual orientation. We have a much better understanding of sexual orientation than we did a couple of decades ago, and within the next decade or two we surely will have an even better understanding. The church might therefore be cautioned not to anchor its policies in yesterday's understandings.

Dave: What do you see happening in various denominations as they continue to wrestle with the topic of homosexuality and the Christian faith?

Letha: You've already pointed out the conflict in your own denomination, Dave. We see such struggles all across the board. The Evangelical Lutheran Church in America recently voted 503–490 to continue its ban on sexually active homosexual clergy. (You can't get more divided than that.) Decisions by the Judicial Council of the United Methodist Church resulted in the defrocking of Beth Stroud, a lesbian pastor, and the reinstatement of a pastor who had been placed on involuntary leave for refusing church membership to a gay man, underscoring the turmoil in that denomination. Dissension over homosexuality continues to plague Presbyterians.

Anglicans are facing a threatened split over the ordination of gays. And the Vatican has just issued a statement that could be interpreted to bar even celibate gay men from entering the Roman Catholic priesthood. Jewish groups are not spared such questions and controversies either. The documentary film, *Trembling Before God,* along with a follow-up DVD on the film's effect around the world, make it clear that even Orthodox Judaism is wrestling with these questions.

Clearly, issues of homosexual persons with regard to ministry and marriage are not going to go away within religious bodies. Two understandings seem to have emerged. Some religious people see homosexuality as nothing more nor less than a type of behavior—a chosen sexual behavior they believe is forbidden in the Bible. Others see homosexuality as a way of *being,* an orientation that is innate and not chosen. As with a heterosexual orientation, a homosexual orientation can be expressed in ways that either honor or dishonor God. In this view, homosexual persons are a *minority* group, not a *deviant* group. Marriage, then, provides both heterosexual and homosexual persons a way to honor God and one's chosen partner through a faithful covenantal love relationship.

Dave: Why does knowing or not knowing a gay or lesbian person affect the feelings people have about homosexual relationships?

Letha: I think when we keep a subject such as homosexuality distant from us, seeing it only in the abstract, it's easy to believe false information, accept stereotypes, and act accordingly. Homosexual people are then seen as an "out-group," a category distinctly different from the heterosexual "in-group." A blind spot makes it hard see gay people as human beings, as *persons* who want the same things as straight people do— to love and belong and just go about their lives with dignity, as persons made in God's image.

But when a heterosexual person learns that what had been only a generalized abstract mental construct is actually *em-*

bodied in an admired person who reveals his or her homosexual orientation, something begins to happen. How can you continue to believe gay relationships don't last after getting to know Pete and Tom, who have been together 50 years, and have watched Pete tenderly caring for Tom, who now suffers from Alzheimer's disease? How can you claim that homosexual people are rejecting God when that life-transforming sermon you can't get out of your mind was preached by a lesbian minister? How can you believe that homosexual people are unfit parents when you see the love and care that Elaine and Laura shower on their baby, or the fun little Joey has as he plays and laughs with his two dads, whom he adores? Meeting gay people replaces an abstract topic with real people and with the universality of human experience.

Letha: Do you have statistics about any recent changes in attitudes toward same-sex marriage?

Dave: Yes. A *Boston Globe* survey of Massachusetts residents showed that support for same-sex marriage increased from 40 to 56 percent in the year following the state's recognition of gay marriage. As so often happens, social attitudes follow social practice (a phenomenon we witnessed in the decades following the 1954 Supreme Court desegregation decision and the 1964 U.S. Civil Rights Act). So far, it looks like heterosexual marriage is not suffering any decline in Massachusetts.

As this paperback edition goes to press, most Americans still oppose same-sex marriage, but they are a declining majority. The combination of changing attitudes and of generational succession suggests that those opposed to same-sex marriage had better get their state constitutional bans passed soon (though if present trends continue, those bans may eventually get overturned).

Letha: We're seeing these changing attitudes all around the globe. In our first edition of this book we mentioned the legalization of marriage in the Netherlands, Belgium, and

Canada. Now Spain has joined the list. And South Africa's highest court ruled in December 2005 that the country's Parliament would have one year to change the wording of its marriage laws or else the law would automatically be changed to utilize gender neutral language. That same month, Britain's Civil Partnership Law went into effect, which will grant all the privileges and responsibilities of marriage to same-sex couples who officially register throughout the UK, although the word "marriage" is not being used.

Dave: Those of us who support "monogamy for all" can take heart that more and more people see the welcoming of gay people into monogamy—into marriage—as a positive trend, while also seeing declines in teen pregnancy and increases in teen abstinence as another positive trend. The bridge across the divide will be constructed, I do believe, as the culture and the church come to adopt a consistent pro-marriage mandate.